Incredibly Easy
Chinese

Publications International, Ltd.
Favorite Brand Name Recipes at www.fbnr.com

Front cover photography and photography on pages 17, 27, 33, 51, 71, 77, 81, 101, 143, 149 and 153 by Tony Glaser Photography.
Photographer: Tony Glaser
Photographer's Assistant: Flint Chaney
Prop Stylist: Diane Arnold
Food Stylist: Josephine Orba
Assistant Food Stylist: Constance Pikulas

Pictured on the front cover: Cashew Beef *(page 58).*
Pictured on the back cover: Savory Pork Stir-Fry *(page 80).*

ISBN-13: 978-1-4127-2533-0
ISBN-10: 1-4127-2533-X

Library of Congress Control Number: 2006929237

Manufactured in China.

8 7 6 5 4 3 2 1

Preparation/Cooking Times: Preparation times are based on the approximate amount of time required to assemble the recipe before cooking, baking, chilling or serving. These times include preparation steps such as measuring, chopping and mixing. The fact that some preparations and cooking can be done simultaneously is taken into account. Preparation of optional ingredients and serving suggestions is not included.

Contents

Chinatown Stuffed
Mushrooms (p. 6)

Asian Pasta & Shrimp Soup
(p. 26)

Chinese Chicken Salad
(p. 16)

Mini Marinated Beef
Skewers (p. 24)

Appetizers, Soups
& Salads

Chinatown Stuffed Mushrooms

24 large fresh mushrooms (about 1 pound), cleaned
½ pound ground turkey
1 clove garlic, minced
¼ cup fine dry bread crumbs
¼ cup thinly sliced green onions
3 tablespoons reduced-sodium soy sauce, divided
1 egg white, lightly beaten
1 teaspoon minced fresh ginger
⅛ teaspoon red pepper flakes (optional)

1. Remove stems from mushrooms; finely chop enough stems to equal 1 cup. Cook turkey with chopped stems and garlic in medium skillet over medium-high heat until turkey is no longer pink, stirring to separate turkey. Spoon off any fat. Stir in bread crumbs, green onions, 2 tablespoons soy sauce, egg white, ginger and pepper flakes, if desired; mix well.

2. Preheat broiler; line broiler pan with foil. Brush mushroom caps lightly on all sides with remaining 1 tablespoon soy sauce; spoon about 2 teaspoons stuffing into each mushroom cap.* Place stuffed mushrooms on rack of prepared pan. Broil 4 to 5 inches from heat 5 to 6 minutes or until hot.   *Makes 24 appetizers*

*Mushrooms may be made ahead to this point; cover and refrigerate up to 24 hours. Add 1 to 2 minutes to broiling time for chilled mushrooms. Or, freeze filling separately in individual portions. To freeze, place portions on cookie sheet or shallow pan; place in freezer 30 minutes to firm slightly. Remove from freezer; place in freezer food storage bag and freeze completely. Thaw in refrigerator before filling mushrooms as directed.

Stir-Fry Beef & Vegetable Soup

Prep and Cook Time: 22 minutes

1 boneless beef top sirloin or top round steak (about 1 pound)
2 teaspoons dark sesame oil, divided
3 cans (about 14 ounces each) reduced-sodium beef broth
1 package (16 ounces) frozen stir-fry vegetables
3 green onions, thinly sliced
¼ cup stir-fry sauce

1. Slice beef lengthwise in half, then crosswise into ⅛-inch-thick strips.

2. Heat Dutch oven or large saucepan over medium-high heat. Add 1 teaspoon oil and tilt pan to coat bottom. Add half of beef in single layer; cook 1 minute, without stirring, until lightly browned on bottom. Turn and brown other side about 1 minute; remove beef from pan. Repeat with remaining 1 teaspoon oil and beef; set aside.

3. Add broth to Dutch oven. Cover; bring to a boil over high heat. Add vegetables. Reduce heat; simmer 3 to 5 minutes or until vegetables are heated through. Add beef, green onions and stir-fry sauce; simmer 1 minute. *Makes 6 servings*

Serving Suggestion: Make a quick sesame bread to serve with the soup. Brush refrigerated dinner roll dough with water, then dip in sesame seeds before baking.

Chicken Salad Canton

Prep Time: 15 minutes

1 cup fresh Chinese snow peas *or* **1 package (6 ounces) frozen snow peas, thawed**

1 can (14½ ounces) DEL MONTE® Stewed Tomatoes - Original Recipe

3 tablespoons vegetable oil

3 tablespoons cider vinegar

1 tablespoon low-salt soy sauce

4 cups shredded cabbage or iceberg lettuce

1 cup cubed cooked chicken

⅓ cup packed cilantro, chopped, *or* **⅓ cup sliced green onions**

1. Dip fresh snow peas in boiling water 30 seconds (do not dip frozen snow peas); cool.

2. Drain tomatoes, reserving ¼ cup liquid. Combine reserved liquid with oil, vinegar and soy sauce.

3. Toss soy dressing and tomatoes with remaining ingredients. Season to taste with pepper, if desired. Garnish with sliced green onions and toasted sesame seeds, if desired.

Makes 2 main-dish servings (4 side-dish servings)

Ginger Plum Spareribs

Prep Time: 15 minutes, plus marinating • **Bake Time:** 1 hour

1 jar (10 ounces) damson plum preserves or apple jelly
⅓ cup KARO® Light or Dark Corn Syrup
⅓ cup soy sauce
¼ cup chopped green onions
2 cloves garlic, minced
2 teaspoons ground ginger
2 pounds country-style pork spareribs, trimmed, cut into
**   serving pieces**

1. In small saucepan combine preserves, corn syrup, soy sauce, green onions, garlic and ginger. Stirring constantly, cook over medium heat until melted and smooth.

2. Pour into 11×7×2-inch baking dish. Add ribs, turning to coat. Cover; refrigerate several hours or overnight, turning once.

3. Remove ribs from marinade; place on rack in shallow baking pan.

4. Bake in 350°F oven about 1 hour or until tender, turning occasionally and basting with marinade.

Makes about 20 appetizer or 4 main-dish servings

Ginger Plum Chicken Wings: Omit spareribs. Follow recipe for Ginger Plum Spareribs. Use 2½ pounds chicken wings, separated at the joints (tips discarded). Bake 45 minutes, basting with marinade during last 30 minutes.

Asian Crab & Noodle Salad

1 package (10 ounces) Chinese curly noodles or 10 ounces vermicelli
1 package (8 ounces) flaked imitation crabmeat
6 ounces (1½ cups) fresh snow peas or sugar snap peas
⅓ cup soy sauce
2 tablespoons seasoned rice vinegar
2 tablespoons dark sesame oil
1 teaspoon minced fresh ginger
½ teaspoon minced garlic
¼ teaspoon red pepper flakes
1 red bell pepper, cut into strips
¼ cup thinly sliced green onions

1. Bring 3 quarts water to a boil in large saucepan over high heat. Add noodles; return to a boil. Cook 2 minutes. Add crabmeat and snow peas; cook 1 minute or until noodles are al dente.

2. Meanwhile, for dressing, combine soy sauce, vinegar, oil, ginger, garlic and red pepper flakes in large bowl; mix well.

3. Drain noodle mixture. Add noodle mixture and bell pepper to dressing; toss to coat. Arrange mixture on salad plates; sprinkle with green onions.

Makes 4 servings

Quick Hot and Sour Chicken Soup

2 cups chicken broth

2 cups water

1 package (about 10 ounces) refrigerated fully cooked chicken breast strips, cut into pieces

1 package (about 7 ounces) reduced-sodium chicken-flavored rice and vermicelli mix

1 large jalapeño pepper,* minced

2 green onions, chopped

1 tablespoon soy sauce

1 tablespoon fresh lime juice

1 tablespoon minced fresh cilantro (optional)

*Jalapeño peppers can sting and irritate the skin, so wear rubber gloves when handling peppers and do not touch your eyes.

1. Combine broth, water, chicken, rice mix, jalapeño pepper, green onions and soy sauce in large saucepan. Bring to a boil over high heat. Reduce heat to low. Cover; simmer 20 minutes or until rice is tender, stirring occasionally.

2. Stir in lime juice; sprinkle with cilantro.   *Makes 4 servings*

Chinese Chicken Salad

4 cups chopped bok choy
3 cups cooked, diced chicken breast (1 pound boneless skinless chicken breast meat)
1 cup shredded carrots
2 tablespoons minced chives or green onions
2 tablespoons hot chili sauce with garlic*
1½ tablespoons peanut or canola oil
1 tablespoon balsamic vinegar
1 tablespoon soy sauce
1 teaspoon minced fresh ginger

Hot chili sauce with garlic is available in the Asian foods section of most supermarkets.

1. Place bok choy, chicken, carrots and chives in serving bowl.

2. Combine chili sauce, oil, vinegar, soy sauce and ginger in small bowl; mix well. Pour over chicken mixture and toss gently.   *Makes 4 servings*

Marinated Cucumbers

1 large cucumber (about 12 ounces)
2 tablespoons rice vinegar
2 tablespoons peanut or vegetable oil
2 tablespoons soy sauce
1½ teaspoons sugar
1 clove garlic, minced
¼ teaspoon red pepper flakes

1. Score cucumber lengthwise with tines of fork. Cut in half lengthwise; scrape out and discard seeds. Cut crosswise into ⅛-inch slices; place in medium bowl.

2. Combine remaining ingredients in small bowl; pour over cucumber and toss to coat. Cover; refrigerate at least 4 hours or up to 2 days.
Makes 4 to 6 servings

Asian Lettuce Wraps

2 cups shredded cabbage or cole slaw mix
2 cups pre-cut vegetables
6 ounces oven roasted or honey baked turkey, diced
⅓ cup dry roasted unsalted peanuts (see Note)
⅓ cup stir-fry sauce
1 to 2 tablespoons honey
12 whole Bibb or Boston lettuce leaves
Whole fresh chives (optional)

1. Combine shredded cabbage, vegetables, turkey and peanuts in medium bowl. Add stir-fry sauce and honey; toss gently until well coated.

2. Place about ½ cup cabbage mixture on each leaf.

3. Fold up bottom and two sides of leaves to form wraps. Tie closed with whole chives, if desired. *Makes 4 servings*

Note: For nuttier flavor, toast peanuts in a small nonstick skillet over medium-high heat 3 minutes or until fragrant and beginning to brown. Remove from skillet immediately.

*Tip

Bibb and Boston lettuce are part of the butterhead lettuce family; sometimes they are referred to as butter lettuce. Butterhead lettuces have small, loose heads which contain soft, tender leaves; they are more delicate than other lettuces and require gentler handling.

Szechuan Chicken Salad with Peanut Dressing

1 pound boneless skinless chicken breast halves
1 can (about 14 ounces) chicken broth
1 tablespoon creamy peanut butter
1 tablespoon peanut or vegetable oil
1 tablespoon soy sauce
1 tablespoon rice vinegar
1 teaspoon dark sesame oil
¼ teaspoon ground red pepper
  Shredded lettuce
  Chopped fresh cilantro or green onions (optional)

1. Place chicken in single layer in large skillet. Pour broth over chicken; bring to a boil over high heat. Reduce heat to medium-low. Cover and simmer 10 to 12 minutes until chicken is no longer pink in center.

2. Meanwhile, mix peanut butter and peanut oil in small bowl until smooth. Stir in soy sauce, rice vinegar, sesame oil and ground red pepper.

3. Drain chicken; reserve broth. Stir 2 tablespoons reserved broth* into peanut butter mixture.

4. To serve salad warm, cut chicken crosswise into ½-inch slices and place on lettuce-lined plates. Spoon peanut dressing over chicken. Sprinkle with cilantro.

5. To serve salad at room temperature, cool chicken and shred or coarsely chop. Toss chicken with peanut dressing; cover and refrigerate. Before serving, bring chicken mixture to room temperature (about 1 hour). Arrange chicken on lettuce-lined plates. Sprinkle with cilantro.

Makes 4 servings

Strain remaining broth; cover and refrigerate or freeze for use in other recipes.

Sweet and Sour Pork Meatballs

Prep Time: 25 minutes

1 pound lean ground pork
¼ cup finely chopped water chestnuts
¼ cup chopped onion
1 egg, slightly beaten
¼ cup soy sauce, divided
⅛ teaspoon ground ginger
1 teaspoon vegetable oil
1 can (8 ounces) pineapple chunks
1 tablespoon vinegar
1 tablespoon cornstarch
1 tablespoon sugar

In large bowl combine pork, water chestnuts, onion, egg, 2 tablespoons soy sauce and ginger; shape into 1-inch balls. In nonstick skillet cook meatballs in hot oil until browned. Remove meatballs and drain on paper towels, reserving drippings in skillet.

Drain pineapple, reserving juice. In 1-cup measure combine pineapple juice, remaining 2 tablespoons soy sauce and vinegar. Add water to equal 1 cup liquid. In mixing bowl combine cornstarch and sugar. Gradually stir in pineapple juice mixture; mix well. Add juice mixture to pan drippings. Cook over medium heat until thickened and bubbly, stirring constantly. Stir in meatballs and reserved pineapple chunks. Cook 4 to 5 minutes or until heated through. *Makes 24 meatballs*

Favorite recipe from **National Pork Board**

Asian Noodle Soup

4 ounces uncooked dried Chinese egg noodles
3 cans (about 14 ounces each) reduced-sodium chicken broth
2 slices fresh ginger
2 cloves garlic, peeled and cut into halves
½ cup fresh snow peas, cut into 1-inch pieces
3 tablespoons chopped green onions
1 tablespoon chopped fresh cilantro
1½ teaspoons hot chili oil
½ teaspoon dark sesame oil

1. Cook noodles according to package directions. Drain and set aside.

2. Combine broth, ginger and garlic in large saucepan; bring to a boil over high heat. Reduce heat to low; simmer about 15 minutes. Remove and discard ginger and garlic.

3. Add snow peas, green onions, cilantro, chili oil and sesame oil to broth; simmer 3 to 5 minutes. Stir in noodles; heat through. Serve immediately. Garnish, if desired. *Makes 4 servings*

Chinese Cabbage Salad

¼ cup rice vinegar or cider vinegar
2 teaspoons minced fresh ginger
2 teaspoons honey or sugar
2 teaspoons dark sesame oil
1 teaspoon reduced-sodium soy sauce
12 to 14 ounces napa cabbage, shredded (6 to 8 cups)
3 green onions, thinly sliced diagonally

Combine vinegar, ginger, honey, oil and soy sauce in large bowl. Add cabbage and green onions; toss to coat. *Makes 6 servings*

Mini Marinated Beef
Skewers

1 boneless beef top sirloin steak (about 1 pound)
2 tablespoons soy sauce
2 tablespoons dry sherry
1 tablespoon dark sesame oil
2 cloves garlic, minced
18 cherry tomatoes
Lettuce leaves (optional)

1. Cut beef crosswise into ⅛-inch slices; place in large resealable food storage bag. Combine soy sauce, sherry, oil and garlic in small bowl; pour over steak. Seal bag; turn to coat. Marinate in refrigerator at least 30 minutes or up to 2 hours. Soak 18 (6-inch) wooden skewers in water 20 minutes.

2. Preheat broiler. Drain steak; discard marinade. Weave beef accordion-fashion onto skewers. Place on rack of broiler pan.

3. Broil 4 to 5 inches from heat 4 minutes. Turn skewers over; broil 4 minutes or until beef is barely pink in center.

4. Garnish each skewer with one cherry tomato; place on lettuce-lined platter. Serve warm or at room temperature.   *Makes 18 appetizers*

Asian Pasta & Shrimp Soup

Prep Time: 10 minutes • **Cook Time:** about 10 minutes

- **1 package (3½ ounces) fresh shiitake mushrooms**
- **2 teaspoons Asian sesame oil**
- **2 cans (14½ ounces each) vegetable broth**
- **½ cup water**
- **4 ounces angel hair pasta, broken into 2-inch lengths (about 1 cup)**
- **½ pound medium shrimp, peeled and deveined**
- **4 ounces snow peas, cut into thin strips**
- **2 tablespoons *French's*® Honey Dijon Mustard**
- **1 tablespoon *Frank's*® *RedHot*® Original Cayenne Pepper Sauce**
- **⅛ teaspoon ground ginger**

1. Remove and discard stems from mushrooms. Cut mushrooms into thin strips. Heat oil in large saucepan over medium-high heat. Add mushrooms; stir-fry 3 minutes or just until tender.

2. Add broth and water to saucepan. Heat to boiling. Stir in pasta. Cook 2 minutes or just until tender.

3. Add remaining ingredients, stirring frequently. Heat to boiling. Reduce heat to medium-low. Cook 2 minutes or until shrimp turn pink and peas are tender.   *Makes 4 servings*

Chicken Fried Rice
(p. 34)

Ginger Plum Chicken
(p. 32)

Simple Chinese Chicken
(p. 42)

Luscious Lo Mein
(p. 50)

Sensational Poultry

Orange Chicken
Stir-Fry

½ **cup orange juice**
2 **tablespoons sesame oil, divided**
2 **tablespoons soy sauce**
1 **tablespoon dry sherry**
2 **teaspoons freshly grated fresh ginger**
1 **teaspoon freshly grated orange peel**
1 **clove garlic, minced**
1½ **pounds boneless skinless chicken breasts, cut into strips**
3 **cups mixed fresh vegetables, such as green bell pepper, red bell pepper, snow peas, carrots, green onions, mushrooms and/or onions**
1 **tablespoon cornstarch**
½ **cup unsalted cashew bits or halves**
3 **cups hot cooked rice**

Combine orange juice, 1 tablespoon oil, soy sauce, sherry, ginger, orange peel and garlic in large glass bowl. Add chicken; marinate in refrigerator 1 hour. Drain chicken, reserving marinade. Heat remaining 1 tablespoon oil in large skillet or wok over medium-high heat. Add chicken; stir-fry 3 minutes or until chicken is light brown. Add vegetables; stir-fry 3 to 5 minutes or until vegetables are crisp-tender. Combine cornstarch and marinade; add to skillet and stir until sauce boils and thickens. Stir in cashews; cook 1 minute more. Serve over hot rice.   *Makes 6 servings*

Favorite recipe from **USA Rice**

Ginger Plum Chicken

Prep Time: 20 minutes • **Cook Time:** 10 to 12 minutes

2 tablespoons cooking oil
1 tablespoon thinly sliced fresh ginger
8 ounces chicken (boneless breast or thigh), cut into strips 1 inch thick
3 tablespoons LEE KUM KEE® Premium Brand or Panda Brand or Choy Sun Oyster Sauce
½ cup red bell pepper, cut into 1-inch cubes
½ cup green bell pepper, cut into 1-inch cubes
½ cup carrots, cut into 1-inch strips
3 tablespoons LEE KUM KEE® Plum Sauce
1 green onion, chopped

1. Heat wok or skillet until hot. Add oil, ginger, chicken and LEE KUM KEE Oyster Sauce; cook until chicken is half done.

2. Add vegetables and LEE KUM KEE Plum Sauce; stir-fry 30 seconds. Add green onion; stir-fry until chicken is cooked through.   *Makes 2 servings*

Kung Po Chicken

1 pound boneless skinless chicken breasts
2 cloves garlic, minced
1 teaspoon hot chili oil
1 tablespoon peanut or vegetable oil
¼ cup reduced-sodium soy sauce
2 teaspoons cornstarch
⅓ cup roasted peanuts
2 green onions, cut into short, thin strips

Cut chicken into 1-inch pieces; toss with garlic and chili oil. Heat large skillet over medium-high heat. Add peanut oil; heat until hot. Add chicken mixture; stir-fry 3 minutes or until no longer pink. Blend soy sauce and cornstarch; add to skillet with peanuts and green onions. Stir-fry 1 minute or until sauce boils and thickens.   *Makes 4 servings*

Chicken Fried Rice

1 bag SUCCESS® Rice
½ pound boneless skinless chicken, cut into ½-inch pieces
½ teaspoon salt
¼ teaspoon pepper
2 tablespoons vegetable oil
1 clove garlic, minced
½ teaspoon grated fresh ginger
2 cups diagonally sliced green onions
1 cup sliced fresh mushrooms
2 tablespoons reduced-sodium soy sauce
1 teaspoon sherry
1 teaspoon Asian-style hot chili sesame oil (optional)

Prepare rice according to package directions.

Sprinkle chicken with salt and pepper; set aside. Heat vegetable oil in large skillet over medium-high heat. Add garlic and ginger; cook and stir 1 minute. Add chicken; stir-fry until no longer pink in center. Add green onions and mushrooms; stir-fry until tender. Stir in soy sauce, sherry and sesame oil. Add rice; heat thoroughly, stirring occasionally.

Makes 6 servings

Chicken Chow Mein

1 pound boneless skinless chicken breasts, cut into thin strips

2 cloves garlic, minced

2 teaspoons vegetable oil, divided

2 tablespoons reduced-sodium soy sauce

2 tablespoons dry sherry

6 ounces (2 cups) fresh snow peas, cut into halves *or* 1 package (6 ounces) frozen snow peas, thawed

3 large green onions, cut diagonally into 1-inch pieces

4 ounces uncooked Chinese egg noodles or vermicelli, cooked and drained

1 teaspoon dark sesame oil (optional)

Cherry tomatoes (optional)

Fresh herbs (optional)

1. Toss chicken and garlic in small bowl.

2. Heat 1 teaspoon vegetable oil in wok or large nonstick skillet over medium-high heat. Add chicken mixture; stir-fry 3 minutes or until chicken is no longer pink. Transfer to medium bowl; toss with soy sauce and sherry.

3. Heat remaining 1 teaspoon vegetable oil in wok. Add snow peas; stir-fry 2 minutes for fresh or 1 minute for frozen snow peas. Add green onions; stir-fry 30 seconds. Add chicken mixture; stir-fry 1 minute.

4. Add noodles to wok; stir-fry 2 minutes or until heated through. Stir in sesame oil, if desired. Garnish with cherry tomatoes and fresh herbs.

Makes 4 servings

Moo Shu Wraps

Prep Time: 15 minutes • **Cook Time:** 15 minutes

2 tablespoons vegetable oil

8 ounces shiitake mushrooms, stems discarded, caps sliced

2 teaspoons bottled or fresh minced garlic

2 teaspoons bottled or fresh minced ginger

1 package JENNIE-O TURKEY STORE® Lean Ground Turkey

1 red or yellow bell pepper, cut into short, thin strips

2 cups coleslaw mix (shredded cabbage and carrots) or sliced napa cabbage

½ cup hoisin sauce

⅓ cup plum sauce or sweet-and-sour sauce

12 (about 7-inch) flour tortillas, warmed

Heat oil in large deep skillet over medium-high heat. Add mushrooms, garlic and ginger; stir-fry 2 minutes. Crumble turkey into skillet; add bell pepper. Cook 5 minutes, stirring occasionally. Add coleslaw mix and hoisin sauce; stir-fry 3 minutes. Spread thin layer of plum sauce evenly over each warm tortilla; top with turkey mixture. Fold bottom of tortilla up over filling, fold sides in and roll up. *Makes 6 servings*

*Tip

To peel fresh ginger, use a paring knife with a sharp blade, taking care to remove only the tough outer skin. (The most flavorful part is just below the surface.) A vegetable peeler can also be used. To mince ginger quickly, cut off a small chunk and put through a garlic press.

Sweet and Spicy Chicken Stir-Fry

Prep Time: 5 minutes • **Cook Time:** 20 minutes

1½ **cups uncooked long-grain white rice**
1 **can (8 ounces) DEL MONTE® Pineapple Chunks In Its
    Own Juice**
4 **boneless, skinless chicken breast halves, cut into
    bite-size pieces**
2 **tablespoons vegetable oil**
1 **large green bell pepper, cut into strips**
¾ **cup sweet and sour sauce**
⅛ **to** ½ **teaspoon red pepper flakes**

1. Cook rice according to package directions.

2. Drain pineapple, reserving ⅓ cup juice.

3. Stir-fry chicken in hot oil in large skillet over medium-high heat until no longer pink in center. Add green pepper and reserved pineapple juice; stir-fry 2 minutes or until tender-crisp.

4. Add sweet and sour sauce, red pepper flakes and pineapple; stir-fry 3 minutes or until heated through.

5. Spoon rice onto serving plate; top with chicken mixture. Garnish, if desired.   *Makes 4 servings*

Easy Asian Chicken

Prep Time: 5 minutes • **Cook Time:** 20 minutes

2 packages (3 ounces each) chicken flavor instant ramen noodles
1 package (10 ounces) frozen broccoli florets, thawed
1 package (9 ounces) frozen baby carrots, thawed
1 pound boneless skinless chicken breasts, cut into thin strips
1 tablespoon vegetable oil
1 can (8 ounces) sliced water chestnuts, drained
¼ cup stir-fry sauce

1. Remove seasoning packets from noodles. Reserve one packet for another use.

2. Bring 4 cups water to a boil in large saucepan. Add noodles, broccoli and carrots. Cook over medium-high heat 5 minutes, stirring occasionally; drain.

3. Heat oil in wok or large nonstick skillet over medium-high heat. Add chicken; stir-fry about 8 minutes or until browned.

4. Stir in noodle mixture, water chestnuts, stir-fry sauce and one seasoning packet; cook until heated through.   *Makes 4 to 6 servings*

Simple Chinese Chicken

3 tablespoons frozen orange juice concentrate, thawed
2 tablespoons reduced-sodium soy sauce
2 tablespoons water
¾ teaspoon cornstarch
¼ teaspoon garlic powder
2 carrots, peeled and cut into ¼-inch-thick slices
1 package (12 ounces) frozen broccoli and cauliflower florets, thawed
2 teaspoons peanut or canola oil
1 pound boneless skinless chicken breasts, cut into bite-size pieces
2 cups hot cooked rice

1. For sauce, combine orange juice concentrate, soy sauce, water, cornstarch and garlic powder in small bowl; mix well.

2. Spray wok or large skillet with nonstick cooking spray. Add carrots; stir-fry over high heat 1 minute. Add broccoli and cauliflower; stir-fry 2 to 3 minutes or until vegetables are crisp-tender. Remove vegetables from wok; set aside.

3. Add oil to wok. Stir-fry chicken in hot oil 2 to 3 minutes or until cooked through. Push chicken up side of wok. Add sauce; cook and stir until boiling. Return vegetables to wok; cook and stir until heated through. Serve over rice. *Makes 4 servings*

*Tip

To cut carrots decoratively, use a citrus stripper or grapefruit spoon to cut four or five grooves into whole carrots, cutting lengthwise from stem end to tip. Then cut carrots crosswise into slices to form flowers.

Peanut Chicken
Stir-Fry

**1 package (6.1 ounces) RICE-A-RONI® With ⅓ Less Salt
Fried Rice**
½ cup reduced-sodium or regular chicken broth
2 tablespoons creamy peanut butter
1 tablespoon reduced-sodium or regular soy sauce
1 tablespoon vegetable oil
**¾ pound skinless, boneless chicken breasts,
cut into ½-inch pieces**
2 cloves garlic, minced
**2 cups frozen mixed carrots, broccoli and red pepper
vegetable medley, thawed, drained**
2 tablespoons chopped peanuts (optional)

1. Prepare Rice-A-Roni® mix as package directs.

2. While Rice-A-Roni® is simmering, combine chicken broth, peanut butter and soy sauce; mix with fork. Set aside.

3. In second large skillet or wok, heat oil over medium-high heat. Stir-fry chicken and garlic 2 minutes.

4. Add vegetables and broth mixture; stir-fry 5 to 7 minutes or until sauce has thickened. Serve over rice. Sprinkle with peanuts, if desired.

Makes 4 servings

Light Chop Suey

Cook Time: 15 minutes

Nonstick cooking spray

4 ounces shiitake mushrooms, stems discarded and caps sliced, *or* 2 cups sliced button mushrooms

2 teaspoons bottled minced garlic

1 package JENNIE-O TURKEY STORE® Extra Lean Ground Turkey

3 tablespoons reduced-sodium soy sauce

1 can (8 ounces) sliced water chestnuts, drained

4 green onions, cut diagonally into ½-inch slices

1 cup chicken broth

1½ tablespoons cornstarch

3 cups hot cooked white rice

½ cup chow mein noodles (optional)

Coat large deep skillet or wok with cooking spray; place over medium heat. Add mushrooms and garlic; stir-fry 2 minutes. Crumble turkey into skillet; add soy sauce. Cook 3 minutes, stirring occasionally. Add water chestnuts and green onions. Combine broth and cornstarch, mixing until smooth. Add to skillet; simmer uncovered 5 minutes or until thickened. Serve over rice; top with noodles, if desired.   *Makes 4 servings*

Cashew Chicken

Prep Time: 15 minutes • **Cook Time:** 15 minutes

1 tablespoon BERTOLLI® Olive Oil
1 pound boneless, skinless chicken breasts, cut into thin strips
1 envelope LIPTON® RECIPE SECRETS® Onion Soup Mix
¾ cup water
¼ cup firmly packed brown sugar
2 tablespoons sherry or water
1 tablespoon soy sauce
⅛ teaspoon ground ginger
1 package (16 ounces) frozen whole green beans, partially thawed
4 cups shredded iceberg lettuce
¼ cup chopped cashews or peanuts

1. In 12-inch nonstick skillet, heat oil over medium-high heat and brown chicken, stirring occasionally, 6 minutes or until chicken is thoroughly cooked. Remove chicken and keep warm.

2. In same skillet, stir in soup mix blended with water, brown sugar, sherry, soy sauce and ginger. Bring to a boil and continue boiling 3 minutes.

3. Add green beans and boil over medium heat 3 minutes. Return chicken to skillet and toss well.

4. To serve, arrange lettuce on serving platter; top with chicken and beans. Sprinkle with cashews.   *Makes 4 servings*

Simple Stir-Fry

1 tablespoon vegetable oil
12 boneless, skinless chicken breast tenderloins, cut into 1-inch pieces
1 bag (1 pound) frozen stir-fry vegetable mix
2 tablespoons soy sauce
2 tablespoons honey
2 (2-cup) bags UNCLE BEN'S® Boil-in-Bag Rice

1. Heat oil in large skillet or wok. Add chicken; cook over medium-high heat 6 to 8 minutes or until lightly browned. Add vegetables, soy sauce and honey. Cover and cook 5 to 8 minutes or until chicken is no longer pink in center and vegetables are crisp-tender.

2. Meanwhile, cook rice according to package directions. Serve stir-fry over rice.   *Makes 4 servings*

Hoisin Chicken Breasts Supreme

½ cup hoisin sauce
3 tablespoons rice wine or sake
2 tablespoons sugar
2 tablespoons low-sodium soy sauce
2 tablespoons ketchup
2 tablespoons minced garlic
2½ pounds boneless skinless chicken breasts

Combine all ingredients except chicken in bowl. Add chicken and turn to coat. Cover and let marinate several hours in refrigerator.

Preheat oven to 375°F. Arrange chicken in large baking pan lined with aluminum foil. Bake for 20 to 25 minutes or until cooked through. Serve whole or cut into strips.   *Makes 8 servings*

Favorite recipe from **The Sugar Association, Inc.**

Luscious Lo Mein

Prep Time: 30 minutes • **Cook Time:** 15 minutes

8 ounces uncooked lo mein or udon noodles or spaghetti
2 tablespoons vegetable oil
1 package JENNIE-O TURKEY STORE® Boneless Breast
Tenderloins, cut into ¾-inch chunks
2 teaspoons bottled or fresh minced ginger
2 teaspoons bottled or fresh minced garlic
¼ teaspoon crushed red pepper flakes
2 cups sliced bok choy or fresh sugar snap peas
1 cup thin red bell pepper strips
¼ cup chicken broth
¼ cup soy sauce or tamari
2 tablespoons oyster sauce
2 tablespoons dark sesame oil

Cook noodles according to package directions. Meanwhile, heat
1 tablespoon vegetable oil in large deep skillet over medium-high
heat. Add turkey, ginger, garlic and pepper flakes; stir-fry 3 minutes.
Transfer to bowl; set aside. Add remaining 1 tablespoon vegetable oil
to skillet. Add bok choy and bell pepper; stir-fry 2 minutes. Add broth,
soy sauce and oyster sauce; bring to a simmer. Add turkey and sesame
oil to skillet; simmer 2 minutes or until turkey is no longer pink in center.
Drain noodles; add to skillet and heat through. Serve in shallow soup
bowls. *Makes 6 servings*

Moo Goo Gai Pan

1 package (1 ounce) dried black Chinese mushrooms
¼ cup reduced-sodium soy sauce
2 tablespoons rice vinegar
3 cloves garlic, minced
1 pound boneless skinless chicken breasts, cut into
 ½-inch strips
½ cup chicken broth
1 tablespoon cornstarch
2 tablespoons peanut or vegetable oil, divided
1 jar (7 ounces) straw mushrooms, drained
3 green onions, cut into 1-inch pieces
 Hot cooked Chinese egg noodles or white rice (optional)

1. Place dried mushrooms in small bowl; cover with warm water. Soak 20 minutes to soften. Drain; squeeze out excess water. Discard stems; slice caps.

2. Combine soy sauce, vinegar and garlic in medium bowl. Add chicken; marinate at room temperature 20 minutes. Blend broth into cornstarch in small bowl until smooth.

3. Heat wok or large skillet over medium-high heat. Add 1 tablespoon oil; heat until hot. Drain chicken; reserve marinade. Add chicken to wok; stir-fry 3 minutes or until no longer pink. Remove chicken from wok.

4. Heat remaining 1 tablespoon oil in wok. Add mushrooms and green onions; stir-fry 1 minute. Stir broth mixture and add to wok with reserved marinade. Cook 1 minute or until sauce boils and thickens.

5. Return chicken and any accumulated juices to wok; heat through. Serve over noodles. *Makes 4 servings*

Szechuan Beef Lo Mein
(p. 74)

Cashew Beef
(p. 58)

Sesame-Garlic Flank Steak
(p. 70)

Beef and Asparagus Stir-Fry
(p. 76)

Sizzling Beef

Green Dragon
Stir-Fry

2 tablespoons vegetable oil, divided
1 pound beef flank steak, very thinly sliced
1 bunch asparagus *or* 8 ounces green beans,
   cut into 2-inch pieces
1 green bell pepper, cut into strips
1 cup julienned carrots
3 large green onions, sliced
1 tablespoon minced fresh ginger
1 clove garlic, minced
¼ cup water
1 tablespoon soy sauce
1 tablespoon TABASCO® brand Green Pepper Sauce
½ teaspoon salt
2 cups hot cooked rice (optional)

Heat 1 tablespoon oil in 12-inch skillet over medium-high heat. Add flank steak; cook until well browned on all sides, stirring frequently. Remove steak to plate with slotted spoon.

Heat remaining 1 tablespoon oil in skillet over medium heat. Add asparagus, green bell pepper, carrots, green onions, ginger and garlic; cook about 3 minutes, stirring frequently. Add water, soy sauce, TABASCO® Green Pepper Sauce, salt and steak; heat to boiling over high heat.

Reduce heat to low; simmer, uncovered, 3 minutes, stirring occasionally. Serve with rice, if desired. *Makes 4 servings*

Note: Stir-fry is also delicious served over ramen or soba noodles.

Cashew Beef

2 tablespoons cooking oil

8 ounces beef (flank steak, skirt steak, top sirloin or fillet mignon), cut into strips ¼ inch thick

3 tablespoons LEE KUM KEE® Premium Brand, Panda Brand or Choy Sun Oyster Sauce

¼ cup *each* red and green bell pepper, cut into 1-inch strips

2 stalks celery, cut into ½-inch slices

½ cup carrots, cut into ½-inch slices

¼ cup small button mushrooms, cut into halves

2 tablespoons LEE KUM KEE® Soy Sauce

1 green onion, chopped

2 tablespoons cashews, toasted (see Tip)

1 tablespoon LEE KUM KEE® Chili Garlic Sauce or Sriracha Chili Sauce

1. Heat wok or skillet over high heat until hot. Add oil, beef and LEE KUM KEE Oyster Sauce; stir-fry until beef is half done.

2. Add bell peppers, celery, carrots, mushrooms and LEE KUM KEE Soy Sauce; stir-fry until vegetables are crisp-tender. Stir in green onion and cashews. Add Chili Garlic Sauce or Sriracha Chili Sauce for spiciness or use as dipping sauce. *Makes 2 servings*

*Tip

Toasting nuts before using them intensifies their flavor and crunch. To toast nuts, heat them in an ungreased wok or skillet over medium heat until golden brown, stirring frequently. Or, spread them on a baking sheet and place in a 350°F oven for 8 to 10 minutes.

Hot and Spicy Onion Beef

2 tablespoons soy sauce, divided
1 tablespoon cornstarch, divided
¾ pound flank steak, thinly sliced across the grain
2 tablespoons dry sherry
1 teaspoon Oriental sesame oil
1 teaspoon chili paste (optional)
2 tablespoons vegetable oil
1 large onion (12 to 14 ounces), sliced vertically
1 teaspoon minced garlic
   Dried whole red chili peppers to taste
1 tablespoon water

Combine 1 tablespoon soy sauce and 1 teaspoon cornstarch in medium bowl. Add beef; stir to coat. Let stand 30 minutes. Combine remaining tablespoon soy sauce, sherry, sesame oil and chili paste in small bowl; set aside. Heat wok or large skillet over medium heat. Add vegetable oil, swirling to coat sides. Add onion, garlic and chili peppers; cook and stir until onion is tender. Add beef; stir-fry 2 minutes or until lightly browned. Add soy sauce mixture and mix well. Combine remaining 2 teaspoons cornstarch and water; add to wok. Cook and stir until sauce boils and thickens.   *Makes about 4 servings*

Favorite recipe from **National Onion Association**

Broccoli Beef Stir-Fry

½ cup beef broth
4 tablespoons HOLLAND HOUSE® Sherry Cooking Wine,
    divided
2 tablespoons soy sauce
1 tablespoon cornstarch
1 teaspoon sugar
2 tablespoons vegetable oil, divided
2 cups fresh broccoli florets
1 cup fresh snow peas
1 red bell pepper, cut into strips
1 pound boneless top round or sirloin steak, slightly frozen,
    cut into thin strips
1 clove garlic, minced
4 cups hot cooked rice

1. For sauce, in small bowl, combine broth, 2 tablespoons cooking wine, soy sauce, cornstarch and sugar. Mix well and set aside. In large skillet or wok, heat 1 tablespoon oil. Stir-fry broccoli, snow peas and bell pepper 1 minute. Add remaining 2 tablespoons cooking wine.

2. Cover; cook 1 to 2 minutes. Remove vegetables from skillet. Heat remaining 1 tablespoon oil; add meat and garlic. Stir-fry 5 minutes or until meat is browned. Add sauce to meat; cook 2 to 3 minutes or until thickened, stirring frequently. Add vegetables and heat through. Serve over rice.   *Makes 4 servings*

Orange Beef

1 pound boneless beef top sirloin or tenderloin steaks
2 cloves garlic, minced
1 teaspoon grated fresh orange peel
2 tablespoons soy sauce
2 tablespoons orange juice
1 tablespoon dry sherry
1 tablespoon cornstarch
1 tablespoon peanut or vegetable oil
2 cups hot cooked white rice
   Orange peel strips or orange slices (optional)

1. Cut beef in half lengthwise, then crosswise into thin slices. Toss with garlic and orange peel in medium bowl.

2. Blend soy sauce, orange juice and sherry into cornstarch in small bowl until smooth.

3. Heat wok or large skillet over medium-high heat. Add oil; heat until hot. Add half of beef mixture; stir-fry 2 to 3 minutes or until beef is barely pink in center. Remove to large bowl. Repeat with remaining beef. Stir soy sauce mixture and add to wok. Cook 30 seconds or until sauce boils and thickens. Serve over rice; garnish with orange peel.   *Makes 4 servings*

Sweet and Sour Beef

1 pound lean ground beef
1 small onion, thinly sliced
2 teaspoons minced fresh ginger
1 package (16 ounces) frozen Asian-style vegetables
6 to 8 tablespoons prepared sweet and sour sauce or sauce from vegetable mix
Hot cooked rice

1. Cook beef, onion and ginger in large skillet over high heat 6 to 8 minutes or until no longer pink, stirring to separate meat. Drain.

2. Stir in frozen vegetables and sauce. Cover and cook 6 to 8 minutes, stirring occasionally, until vegetables are heated through. Serve over rice.

Makes 4 servings

Black Bean and Chili Garlic Beef

Prep Time: 20 minutes • **Cook Time:** 10 minutes

2 tablespoons cooking oil
8 ounces beef (top sirloin, skirt steak, flank steak or fillet mignon), cut into strips ¼ inch thick
2 tablespoons LEE KUM KEE® Black Bean Garlic Sauce
¼ cup sliced celery
¼ cup small button mushrooms, cut into halves
¼ cup sliced carrots
1 tablespoon LEE KUM KEE® Chili Garlic Sauce
1 green onion, chopped
1 tablespoon LEE KUM KEE® Pure Sesame Oil

1. Heat wok or skillet over high heat until hot. Add cooking oil, beef and LEE KUM KEE Black Bean Garlic Sauce; cook until beef is half done.

2. Add celery, mushrooms, carrots and LEE KUM KEE Chili Garlic Sauce; stir-fry until beef is done. Sprinkle with green onions and LEE KUM KEE Pure Sesame Oil.

Makes 2 servings

Quick 'n' Tangy Beef Stir-Fry

Prep Time: 10 minutes • **Cook Time:** about 10 minutes

Sauce

½ cup *French's*® **Worcestershire Sauce**

½ cup water

2 tablespoons sugar

2 teaspoons cornstarch

½ teaspoon ground ginger

½ teaspoon garlic powder

Stir-Fry

1 tablespoon oil

1 pound thinly sliced beef steak

3 cups sliced bell peppers

1. Combine ingredients for sauce. Marinate beef in ¼ *cup* sauce 5 minutes. Heat oil in large skillet or wok over high heat. Stir-fry beef in batches 5 minutes or until browned.

2. Add peppers; cook 2 minutes. Add remaining sauce; stir-fry until sauce thickens. Serve over hot cooked ramen noodles or rice, if desired.

Makes 4 servings

*Tip

When stir-frying, it's best to cook the beef in batches rather than all at once (unless it's a very small amount). Cooking a large quantity of beef at one time results in the pan and the oil becoming too cool, so the beef will braise and steam rather than fry.

Beef Kabobs in Chinese BBQ (Char Siu) Sauce

Prep Time: 20 to 25 minutes • **Cook Time:** 15 minutes

¼ **cup LEE KUM KEE® Soy Sauce**
¼ **cup LEE KUM KEE® Chinese BBQ Sauce (Char Siu Sauce)**
2 **tablespoons LEE KUM KEE® Chili Garlic Sauce**
2 **tablespoons LEE KUM KEE® Sesame Oil**
1 **pound beef (top sirloin, New York strip or fillet mignon), cut into 1-inch cubes**
12 **cherry tomatoes**
8 **mushrooms**
½ **cup green chili pepper, cut into 1-inch cubes**
1 **large onion, cut into 1-inch cubes**
1 **can (8 ounces) pineapple chunks, drained**

1. For marinade, combine LEE KUM KEE Soy Sauce, Chinese BBQ Sauce, Chili Garlic Sauce and Sesame Oil. Reserve half of marinade. Add beef to remaining half and marinate for 1 hour.

2. Drain beef, discarding marinade. Alternately thread beef, cherry tomatoes, mushrooms, green chili pepper, onion and pineapple chunks onto metal skewers. Preheat grill or broiler.

3. Grill or broil kabobs for 5 to 7 minutes, brushing occasionally with reserved marinade. Turn kabobs over and grill 5 to 7 minutes more or until done. *Makes 4 servings*

Tomato Ginger Beef

Prep Time: 10 minutes • **Cook Time:** 12 minutes

2 tablespoons dry sherry
1 tablespoon soy sauce
2 cloves garlic, crushed
1 teaspoon minced gingerroot *or* **¼ teaspoon ground
   ginger**
1 pound flank steak, thinly sliced
1 tablespoon cornstarch
1 tablespoon vegetable oil
**1 can (14½ ounces) DEL MONTE® Diced Tomatoes
   with Garlic & Onion**
   Hot cooked rice

1. Combine sherry, soy sauce, garlic and ginger; toss with meat. Stir in cornstarch; mix well.

2. Cook meat mixture in oil in large skillet over high heat until browned, stirring constantly.

3. Add tomatoes; cook over high heat until thickened, stirring frequently, about 5 minutes. Serve over hot cooked rice. Garnish with sliced green onions, if desired.   *Makes 4 to 6 servings*

Hint: Partially freeze meat for easier slicing.

Sesame-Garlic Flank Steak

1 beef flank steak (about 1¼ pounds)
2 tablespoons soy sauce
2 tablespoons hoisin sauce
1 tablespoon dark sesame oil
2 cloves garlic, minced

1. Score steak lightly with sharp knife in diamond pattern on both sides; place in resealable food storage bag.

2. Combine remaining ingredients in small bowl; pour over steak. Seal bag; turn to coat. Marinate in refrigerator at least 2 hours or up to 24 hours, turning once.

3. Drain steak; reserve marinade. Grill or broil over medium heat 13 to 18 minutes for medium-rare to medium or until desired doneness, brushing with marinade and turning once halfway through cooking time. Discard remaining marinade. Transfer steak to cutting board; cut into thin slices across the grain. *Makes 4 servings*

Stir-Fried Beef & Spinach

1 package (6 ounces) fresh spinach, stemmed and torn
⅛ teaspoon salt
½ pound boneless beef top sirloin steak, thinly sliced
¼ cup stir-fry sauce
1 teaspoon sugar
½ teaspoon curry powder
¼ teaspoon ground ginger

1. Coat wok or large skillet with nonstick cooking spray. Heat over high heat until hot. Add spinach; stir-fry 1 minute or until limp. Transfer spinach to serving platter; sprinkle with salt and cover to keep warm.

2. Wipe out wok with paper towel; coat with cooking spray. Heat over high heat until hot. Add beef; stir-fry 2 minutes or until barely pink. Add sauce, sugar, curry powder and ginger; cook and stir 1½ minutes or until sauce thickens. Spoon beef mixture over spinach. *Makes 2 servings*

Three-Pepper Steak

1 boneless beef top round or beef flank steak
  (about 1 pound)
3 tablespoons reduced-sodium soy sauce
1 tablespoon cornstarch
1 tablespoon brown sugar
1½ teaspoons sesame oil
¼ teaspoon red pepper flakes
3 tablespoons vegetable oil, divided
1 small green bell pepper, cut into ½-inch strips
1 small red bell pepper, cut into ½-inch strips
1 small yellow bell pepper, cut into ½-inch strips
1 medium onion, cut into 1-inch pieces
2 cloves garlic, finely chopped
  Hot cooked rice

1. Cut beef in half lengthwise, then crosswise into ¼-inch-thick slices. Combine soy sauce, cornstarch, brown sugar, sesame oil and red pepper flakes in medium bowl; stir until smooth. Add beef and toss to coat.

2. Heat wok over high heat about 1 minute or until hot. Drizzle 1 tablespoon vegetable oil into wok and heat 30 seconds. Add bell peppers; stir-fry until crisp-tender. Remove to large bowl. Add 1 tablespoon vegetable oil and heat 30 seconds. Add half of beef mixture to wok; stir-fry until well browned. Remove beef to bowl with bell peppers. Repeat with remaining 1 tablespoon vegetable oil and beef mixture. Reduce heat to medium.

3. Add onion; stir-fry about 3 minutes or until softened. Add garlic; stir-fry 30 seconds. Return bell peppers, beef and any accumulated juices to wok; cook until heated through. Spoon rice into serving dish; top with beef and vegetable mixture. *Makes 4 servings*

Szechuan Beef Lo Mein

1 boneless beef top sirloin steak (about 1 pound)
4 cloves garlic, minced
2 teaspoons minced fresh ginger
¾ teaspoon red pepper flakes, divided
1 tablespoon vegetable oil
1 can (about 14 ounces) vegetable broth
1 cup water
2 tablespoons reduced-sodium soy sauce
1 package (8 ounces) frozen mixed vegetables for stir-fry
1 package (9 ounces) refrigerated angel hair pasta
¼ cup chopped fresh cilantro (optional)

1. Cut beef in half lengthwise, then crosswise into thin slices. Toss beef with garlic, ginger and ½ teaspoon red pepper flakes.

2. Heat oil in large nonstick skillet over medium-high heat. Add half of beef to skillet; stir-fry 2 minutes or until meat is barely pink in center. Remove from skillet; set aside. Repeat with remaining beef.

3. Add broth, water, soy sauce and remaining ¼ teaspoon red pepper flakes to skillet; bring to a boil over high heat. Add vegetables; return to a boil. Reduce heat to low; cover and simmer 3 minutes or until vegetables are crisp-tender.

4. Stir in pasta; return to a boil over high heat. Reduce heat to medium; simmer, uncovered, 2 minutes, stirring to separate pasta. Return beef and any accumulated juices to skillet; simmer 1 minute or until pasta is tender and beef is heated through. Sprinkle with cilantro, if desired.

Makes 4 servings

Beef and Asparagus Stir-Fry

¾ cup water
3 tablespoons soy sauce
3 tablespoons hoisin sauce
1 tablespoon cornstarch
1 tablespoon peanut or vegetable oil
1 pound sirloin steak, cut into thin strips
1 teaspoon dark sesame oil
8 shiitake mushrooms, stems removed and caps thinly
    sliced
1 cup baby corn
8 ounces asparagus (8 to 10 medium spears), trimmed
    and cut into 1-inch pieces
1 cup sugar snap peas or snow peas
½ cup red bell pepper strips
½ cup cherry tomato halves (optional)

1. Whisk together water, soy sauce, hoisin sauce and cornstarch in small bowl; set aside.

2. Heat peanut oil in wok or large skillet over medium-high heat. Add beef; cook and stir 5 to 6 minutes or until still slightly pink. Remove beef to plate with slotted spoon.

3. Add sesame oil, mushrooms and baby corn to wok; cook and stir 2 to 3 minutes or until mushrooms are tender and corn is heated through. Add asparagus, snap peas and bell pepper strips; cook and stir 1 minute or until crisp-tender.

4. Return beef with any juices to skillet. Stir in reserved soy sauce mixture and tomatoes, if desired. Cook 1 minute or until heated through and liquid has thickened, stirring occasionally.   *Makes 4 servings*

One Pan Pork Fu Yung
(p. 98)

Barbecued Pork
(p. 90)

Chinese Pork & Vegetable
Stir-Fry (p. 100)

Spicy Hunan Ribs
(p. 84)

Perfect **Pork**

Savory Pork Stir-Fry

Prep Time: 20 minutes

1 pound lean boneless pork loin
1 tablespoon vinegar
1 tablespoon soy sauce
1 teaspoon sesame oil
1 clove garlic, minced
½ teaspoon ground ginger
1 teaspoon vegetable oil
1 (10-ounce) package frozen stir-fry vegetables, unthawed
1 tablespoon chicken broth or water
    Hot cooked rice (optional)
1 tablespoon toasted sesame seeds (optional)

Slice pork across grain into ⅛-inch strips. Marinate in vinegar, soy sauce, sesame oil, garlic and ginger for 10 minutes. Heat vegetable oil in nonstick pan until hot. Add pork mixture and stir-fry for 3 to 5 minutes, until pork is no longer pink. Add vegetables and chicken broth. Stir mixture, cover and steam until vegetables are crisp-tender. Serve over hot cooked rice and sprinkle with toasted sesame seeds, if desired.   *Makes 4 servings*

Favorite recipe from **National Pork Board**

Chinese-Style Fried Brown Rice

3½ cups water
  2 cups uncooked long-grain brown rice
  3 tablespoons vegetable oil, divided
  2 eggs, lightly beaten
  1 medium yellow onion, coarsely chopped
  1 slice (8 ounces) smoked or baked ham, cut into thin strips
  1 cup frozen green peas, thawed
  1 to 2 tablespoons soy sauce
  1 tablespoon dark sesame oil
  Fresh cilantro (optional)

1. Combine water and rice in medium saucepan. Cover and bring to a boil over high heat. Reduce heat to low; simmer about 40 minutes or until tender and all water is absorbed, stirring occasionally. Remove from heat and let stand, covered, 10 minutes.

2. Fluff rice with fork and spread out on greased baking sheet. Cool to room temperature, about 30 to 40 minutes.

3. Heat wok or large skillet over medium heat about 30 seconds or until hot. Drizzle 1 tablespoon vegetable oil into wok; heat 15 seconds. Add eggs; cook 1 minute or just until set. Turn over and stir to scramble until eggs are cooked but not dry. Remove eggs to bowl.

4. Add remaining 2 tablespoons vegetable oil to wok; heat 30 seconds or until hot. Add onion; stir-fry over medium-high heat about 3 minutes or until tender. Stir in ham; stir-fry 1 minute. Add cooked rice, peas, soy sauce and sesame oil; cook 5 minutes, stirring frequently. Stir in eggs and cook until heated through. Transfer to warm serving dish. Garnish with cilantro. Serve immediately. *Makes 6 servings*

Spicy Hunan Ribs

Prep Time: 5 minutes • **Cook Time:** 3 hours • **Marinate Time:** 1 hour

**1⅓ cups hoisin sauce or *Cattlemen's*® Golden Honey
    Barbecue Sauce**
**⅔ cup *Frank's*® *RedHot*® XTRA Hot Cayenne Pepper Sauce
    or *Frank's*® *RedHot*® Cayenne Pepper Sauce**
¼ cup soy sauce
2 tablespoons brown sugar
2 tablespoons dark sesame oil
2 tablespoons grated peeled ginger root
4 cloves garlic, crushed through a press
2 full racks pork spareribs, trimmed (about 6 pounds)

1. Combine hoisin sauce, XTRA Hot Sauce, soy sauce, brown sugar, sesame oil, ginger and garlic; mix well.

2. Place ribs into large resealable plastic food storage bags. Pour 1½ cups sauce mixture over ribs. Seal bags and marinate in refrigerator 1 to 3 hours or overnight.

3. Prepare grill for indirect cooking over medium-low heat (250°F). Place ribs on rib rack or in foil pan; discard marinade. Cook on covered grill 2½ to 3 hours until very tender. Baste with remaining sauce during last 15 minutes of cooking. If desired, grill ribs over direct heat at end of cooking to char slightly.   *Makes 4 to 6 servings*

*Tip
Use Kansas City or St. Louis-style ribs for this recipe.

Sweet and Sour Pork

Prep Time: 5 minutes • **Cook Time:** 15 to 18 minutes

¾ pound boneless pork
1 teaspoon vegetable oil
1 bag (16 ounces) BIRDS EYE® frozen Pepper Stir Fry
    vegetables
1 tablespoon water
1 jar (14 ounces) sweet and sour sauce
1 can (8 ounces) pineapple chunks, drained

• Cut pork into thin strips.

• In large skillet, heat oil over medium-high heat.

• Add pork; stir-fry until pork is browned.

• Add vegetables and water; cover and cook over medium heat 5 to 7 minutes or until vegetables are crisp-tender.

• Uncover; stir in sweet and sour sauce and pineapple. Cook until heated through. *Makes 4 servings*

Serving Suggestion: Serve over hot cooked rice.

Pork Wraps with Plum Sauce

¼ cup soy sauce
2 tablespoons cornstarch
2 large cloves garlic, peeled and minced
¼ teaspoon freshly ground black pepper
¾ pound boneless stir-fry-cut pork (see Note)
3 tablespoons CRISCO® Oil*, divided
3 eggs, lightly beaten
7 to 8 shiitake mushrooms, stems removed, thinly sliced (or ½ ounce dried—see Note)
4 thinly sliced green onions
2 cups thinly sliced cabbage
⅓ cup plum sauce
8 (6-inch) flour tortillas

*Use your favorite Crisco Oil.

1. Combine soy sauce, cornstarch, garlic and pepper in bowl. Add pork; marinate 15 minutes.

2. Heat 1 tablespoon oil in large skillet or wok on medium-high heat. Add eggs and stir-fry until firm, breaking into small pieces. Remove from pan. Add remaining 2 tablespoons oil to pan. Add marinated pork; stir-fry 3 minutes or until pork is no longer pink. Add mushrooms, green onions and cabbage; stir-fry 2 to 3 minutes or until cabbage is wilted. Stir in eggs.

3. To serve, spread plum sauce down center of each tortilla; place pork mixture on plum sauce. Tuck one edge over filling and roll tightly to enclose filling. Serve immediately.   *Makes 4 servings*

Note: Most supermarkets now carry pork already cut for stir-frying. If not available, use boneless pork loin. Cut into ¼-inch slices and then into ½-inch strips. The recipe can also be prepared with boneless, skinless chicken breasts, cut into thin slivers.

Note: If using dried shiitakes, pour very hot tap water over mushrooms while pork marinates. Keep submerged with the back of a spoon. Soak 10 minutes. Drain. Squeeze out extra moisture. Discard stems and slice caps thinly.

Mandarin Pork Stir-Fry

Prep Time: 15 minutes • **Cook Time:** 15 minutes

1½ cups DOLE® Pineapple Orange or Pineapple Juice, divided
  Vegetable cooking spray
12 ounces lean pork tenderloin, chicken breast or turkey
  tenderloin, cut into thin strips
1 tablespoon finely chopped fresh ginger *or* **½ teaspoon**
  ground ginger
2 cups DOLE® Shredded Carrots
½ cup chopped DOLE® Pitted Prunes or Chopped Dates
4 green onions, cut into 1-inch pieces
2 tablespoons low-sodium soy sauce
1 teaspoon cornstarch

• Heat 2 tablespoons juice over medium-high heat in large nonstick skillet sprayed with vegetable cooking spray until juice bubbles.

• Add pork and ginger; cook and stir 3 minutes or until pork is no longer pink. Remove pork from skillet.

• Heat 3 more tablespoons juice in skillet; add carrots, prunes and green onions. Cook and stir 3 minutes.

• Stir soy sauce and cornstarch into remaining juice; add to carrot mixture. Stir in pork; cover and cook 2 minutes until heated through.

Makes 4 servings

Barbecued Pork

¼ **cup soy sauce**
2 **tablespoons dry red wine**
1 **tablespoon brown sugar**
1 **tablespoon honey**
2 **teaspoons red food coloring (optional)**
1 **green onion, cut in half**
1 **clove garlic, minced**
½ **teaspoon ground cinnamon**
2 **whole pork tenderloins (about 12 ounces each), trimmed**
Hot cooked rice (optional)

1. Combine soy sauce, wine, sugar, honey, food coloring, green onion, garlic and cinnamon in large bowl. Add pork; turn to coat completely. Cover and refrigerate 1 hour or overnight, turning pork occasionally.

2. Preheat oven to 350°F. Drain pork, reserving marinade. Place pork on wire rack set in baking pan. Bake 45 minutes or until thermometer inserted into center of pork registers 160°F, turning and basting frequently with reserved marinade during first 30 minutes of cooking.

3. Remove pork from oven; cool. Cut into diagonal slices. Serve with rice, if desired. *Makes about 6 servings*

Moo Shu Pork

Prep Time: 10 minutes • **Marinate Time:** 15 minutes
Cook Time: 10 minutes

1 cup DOLE® Pineapple Juice
1 tablespoon low-sodium soy sauce
2 teaspoons sesame oil
2 teaspoons cornstarch
8 ounces pork tenderloin, cut into thin strips
1½ cups Oriental-style mixed vegetables
¼ cup hoisin sauce (optional)
8 (8-inch) flour tortillas, warmed
2 green onions, cut into thin strips

• Stir juice, soy sauce, sesame oil and cornstarch in shallow, nonmetallic dish until blended; remove ½ cup mixture for sauce.

• Add pork to remaining juice mixture in shallow dish. Cover and marinate 15 minutes in refrigerator. Drain pork; discard marinade.

• Cook and stir pork in large nonstick skillet over medium-high heat 2 minutes or until pork is lightly browned. Add vegetables; cook and stir 3 to 4 minutes or until vegetables are tender-crisp. Stir in reserved ½ cup juice mixture; cook 1 minute or until sauce thickens.

• Spread hoisin sauce onto center of each tortilla, if desired; top with moo shu pork. Sprinkle with green onions. Fold opposite sides of tortilla over filling; fold remaining sides of tortilla over filling. Garnish, if desired.

Makes 4 servings

Pork Fried Rice

Prep and Cook Time: 30 minutes

2½ cups uncooked long-grain white rice
4 pork chops, diced
2 tablespoons vegetable oil
1 medium onion, finely chopped
1 can (14½ ounces) DEL MONTE® Peas and Carrots, drained
3 green onions, sliced
3 to 4 tablespoons soy sauce

1. Cook rice according to package directions.

2. Cook meat in hot oil in large skillet or wok until no longer pink in center, stirring occasionally. Add chopped onion; cook until tender.

3. Stir in rice, peas and carrots, green onions and soy sauce; heat through, stirring frequently. Season with pepper, if desired.   *Makes 4 servings*

Szechuan Pork & Vegetables

4 butterflied pork loin chops, ½ inch thick (1 to 1¼ pounds)
¼ cup plus 1 tablespoon stir-fry sauce, divided
¾ teaspoon minced fresh ginger *or* ½ teaspoon ground ginger
1 package (16 ounces) frozen Asian-style vegetables, thawed
1 can (5 ounces) crisp chow mein noodles
2 tablespoons chopped green onion

1. Heat large, deep nonstick skillet over medium heat; add pork. Spoon 1 tablespoon stir-fry sauce over pork; sprinkle with ginger. Cook 3 minutes. Turn pork; cook 3 minutes. Remove from skillet.

2. Add vegetables and remaining ¼ cup stir-fry sauce to skillet. Cook over medium-low heat 3 minutes; add pork. Cook 3 minutes or until pork is barely pink in center, stirring vegetables and turning pork once.

3. Arrange chow mein noodles on four serving plates; top with vegetable mixture and pork. Sprinkle with green onion.   *Makes 4 servings*

Citrus Spiced Pork Lo Mein

Prep Time: 15 minutes • **Total Time:** 25 minutes

- **6 ounces linguine**
- **4 teaspoons HERB-OX® chicken flavored bouillon, divided**
- **8 ounces pork tenderloin, halved lengthwise and cut into ¼-inch strips**
- **2 teaspoons vegetable oil**
- **2 cups sliced bok choy**
- **¾ cup water**
- **¼ cup orange juice**
- **2 tablespoons soy sauce**
- **2 teaspoons sesame oil**
- **½ teaspoon red pepper flakes**
- **1 (11-ounce) can mandarin oranges, drained**

Cook noodles according to package directions, adding 2 teaspoons bouillon to cooking liquid. Meanwhile in wok or large skillet, stir-fry pork in hot vegetable oil for 3 minutes. Add bok choy and cook for 3 to 4 minutes more or until pork is cooked through and bok choy is crisp-tender. Add water, orange juice, remaining bouillon, soy sauce, sesame oil and red pepper flakes to pork mixture. Bring to a boil. Stir in cooked noodles; cook and stir for 1 minute. Remove from heat and gently stir in oranges. *Makes 4 servings*

Pork and Red Chili Stir-Fry

Prep Time: 15 minutes

1 pound lean boneless pork loin, cut into thin slices
1 teaspoon vegetable oil
2 cloves garlic, minced
**¾ pound fresh green beans, cut into 2-inch lengths *or*
    1 (10-ounce) package frozen cut green beans, thawed**
2 teaspoons sugar
2 teaspoons soy sauce
**2 small red chili peppers, thinly sliced *or* ½ teaspoon red
    pepper flakes**
**1 teaspoon shredded fresh ginger *or* ½ teaspoon ground
    ginger**
1 teaspoon sesame oil
1 teaspoon rice vinegar

Heat vegetable oil in nonstick skillet. Add pork and garlic; cook and stir until lightly browned. Add green beans; stir-fry until beans and pork are tender, about 5 minutes. Push meat and beans to one side of skillet. Add sugar, soy sauce, chili peppers and ginger; stir to dissolve sugar. Add sesame oil and vinegar. Stir to coat meat and beans. Serve immediately with cooked rice or shredded lettuce.   *Makes 4 servings*

Favorite recipe from **National Pork Board**

One Pan Pork Fu Yung

1 cup reduced-sodium chicken broth
1 tablespoon cornstarch
½ teaspoon dark sesame oil, divided
2 teaspoons canola oil
½ pound boneless pork tenderloin, chopped
5 green onions, thinly sliced, divided
1 cup sliced mushrooms
¼ teaspoon salt
¼ teaspoon white pepper
1 cup bean sprouts
2 eggs
2 egg whites

1. Combine broth, cornstarch and ¼ teaspoon sesame oil in small pan. Cook and stir over medium heat about 5 minutes or until sauce thickens.

2. Heat canola oil in 12-inch nonstick skillet over medium-high heat. Add pork; stir-fry about 4 minutes or until no longer pink.

3. Reserve 2 tablespoons green onion. Add remaining green onions, ¼ teaspoon sesame oil, mushrooms, salt and pepper to skillet; stir-fry 4 to 5 minutes or until lightly browned. Add sprouts; stir-fry about 1 minute. Flatten mixture in skillet with spatula.

4. Beat eggs and egg whites in medium bowl; pour over pork mixture in skillet. Reduce heat to low. Cover; cook about 3 minutes or until eggs are set.

5. Cut into 4 wedges. Top each wedge with ¼ cup sauce and sprinkle with reserved green onion. *Makes 4 servings*

Serving Suggestion: Serve with a lettuce wrap salad. Separate Boston lettuce leaves and arrange on a platter with grated carrot, radish slices, seedless cucumber rounds, red bell pepper strips and bean sprouts. Serve with a dipping sauce made by whisking together 1 cup reduced-sodium chicken broth, 1 tablespoon rice vinegar, ¼ teaspoon dark sesame oil, ¼ teaspoon minced fresh ginger and ¼ teaspoon minced garlic.

Chinese Pork & Vegetable Stir-Fry

2 tablespoons BERTOLLI® Olive Oil, divided
**1 pound pork tenderloin or boneless beef sirloin,
   cut into ¼-inch slices**
6 cups assorted fresh vegetables*
1 can (8 ounces) sliced water chestnuts, drained
1 envelope LIPTON® Recipe Secrets® Onion Soup Mix
¾ cup water
½ cup orange juice
1 tablespoon soy sauce
¼ teaspoon garlic powder

Use any of the following to equal 6 cups: broccoli florets, snow peas, thinly sliced red or green bell peppers or thinly sliced carrots.

In 12-inch skillet, heat 1 tablespoon oil over medium-high heat; brown pork. Remove and set aside.

In same skillet, heat remaining 1 tablespoon oil and cook assorted fresh vegetables, stirring occasionally, 5 minutes. Stir in water chestnuts, onion soup mix blended with water, orange juice, soy sauce and garlic powder. Bring to a boil over high heat. Reduce heat to low and simmer, uncovered, 3 minutes. Return pork to skillet and cook 1 minute or until heated through.   *Makes about 4 servings*

*Tip
Pick up pre-sliced vegetables from your local salad bar.

Sesame Pork with Broccoli

1 pound pork tenderloin, trimmed
1 can (14½ ounces) chicken broth
2 tablespoons cornstarch
1 tablespoon soy sauce
4 green onions with tops, finely chopped
1 tablespoon vegetable oil
1 clove garlic, minced
1½ pounds fresh broccoli, cut into bite-size pieces (about 7 cups)
2 tablespoons sliced pimiento, drained
Hot cooked rice (optional)
2 tablespoons sesame seeds, lightly toasted

Combine chicken broth, cornstarch and soy sauce in small bowl; blend well. Stir in green onions; set aside. Cut pork tenderloin lengthwise into quarters; cut each quarter into bite-size pieces. Heat oil in wok or heavy skillet over medium-high heat. Add pork and garlic; stir-fry 3 to 4 minutes or until pork is tender. Remove pork; keep warm. Stir broth mixture; add to wok with broccoli. Cover and simmer over low heat 8 minutes. Add cooked pork and pimiento to wok; cook just until mixture is hot, stirring frequently. Serve over rice, if desired. Sprinkle with sesame seeds. Garnish as desired. *Makes 6 servings*

Favorite recipe from **National Pork Board**

Fried Noodle and Pork Stir-Fry

Noodle Bundles (recipe follows)
½ cup stir-fry sauce
¼ cup red wine
1 teaspoon hot pepper sauce
½ teaspoon cornstarch
2 tablespoons peanut oil, divided
¾ pound boneless pork tenderloin, cut into thin pieces
1 carrot, thinly sliced
1 medium onion, chopped
2 stalks celery, thinly sliced
1 medium red bell pepper, cut into thin strips

1. Prepare Noodle Bundles; set aside and keep warm.

2. Combine stir-fry sauce, wine, hot pepper sauce and cornstarch in small bowl.

3. Heat 1 tablespoon oil in wok or large skillet over high heat. Add pork; stir-fry 3 minutes and remove from wok. Add remaining 1 tablespoon oil and carrot to wok; stir-fry 1 minute. Add onion, celery and bell pepper; stir-fry 3 minutes or until vegetables are tender.

4. Return pork to wok; add sauce mixture. Cook and stir until mixture boils and sauce is slightly thickened. Serve over Noodle Bundles.

Makes 4 to 6 servings

Noodle Bundles: Cook 8 ounces vermicelli or thin spaghetti according to package directions; rinse and drain. Arrange noodles in 4 to 6 bundles. Heat 1 tablespoon peanut oil in large nonstick skillet over medium-high heat. Add 2 to 3 bundles to skillet; cook 5 minutes or until bottom of bundles are golden. Repeat with remaining bundles, adding more oil to pan as needed.

Hot & Sour Shrimp
(p. 126)

Seafood & Vegetable
Stir-Fry (p. 118)

Orange Almond Scallops
(p. 113)

Beijing Fillet of Sole
(p. 116)

Seafood Treasures

Savoy
Shrimp

1 pound large shrimp (about 20), peeled, tail on
½ teaspoon Chinese five-spice powder*
2 tablespoons dark sesame oil
4 cups sliced savoy or Napa cabbage
1 cup snow peas, trimmed
1 tablespoon reduced-sodium soy sauce
1 tablespoon diced candied ginger (optional)
1 teaspoon red pepper flakes
½ teaspoon ground ginger
Juice of 1 lime
¼ cup chopped fresh cilantro

Chinese five-spice powder is a blend of cinnamon, cloves, fennel seed, anise and Szechuan peppercorns. It is available in most supermarkets and at Asian grocery stores.

1. Rinse and drain shrimp. Toss with Chinese five-spice powder until evenly coated.

2. Heat oil in wok or large nonstick skillet over medium heat. Add cabbage, snow peas, soy sauce, candied ginger, red pepper flakes and ground ginger; stir-fry until cabbage is tender.

3. Stir in shrimp and lime juice. Reduce heat to low; cover and cook 3 minutes or until shrimp are pink and opaque. Sprinkle with cilantro.

Makes 4 servings

Noodles with Baby Shrimp

1 package (3.75 ounces) bean thread noodles
1 tablespoon vegetable oil
3 green onions, cut into 1-inch pieces
1 package (16 ounces) frozen mixed vegetables
    (such as cauliflower, broccoli and carrots)
1 cup vegetable broth
8 ounces frozen baby shrimp
1 tablespoon soy sauce
2 teaspoons dark sesame oil
¼ teaspoon black pepper

1. Place noodles in large bowl. Cover with hot tap water; let stand 10 to 15 minutes or just until softened. Drain noodles and cut into 5- or 6-inch pieces; set aside.

2. Heat wok over high heat about 1 minute or until hot. Drizzle vegetable oil into wok and heat 30 seconds. Add green onions; stir-fry 1 minute. Add mixed vegetables; stir-fry 2 minutes. Add broth; bring to a boil. Reduce heat to low; cover and cook about 5 minutes or until vegetables are crisp-tender.

3. Add shrimp to wok and cook just until thawed. Stir in noodles, soy sauce, sesame oil and pepper; stir-fry until heated through.

Makes 4 to 6 servings

Grilled Oriental Salmon with Plum Sauce

Prep Time: 10 minutes • **Cook Time:** 10 minutes

1 pound salmon fillets
3 tablespoons LEE KUM KEE® Soy Sauce
2 tablespoons margarine or butter
3 tablespoons LEE KUM KEE® Plum Sauce
2 tablespoons LEE KUM KEE® Sriracha Chili Sauce

1. Marinate salmon in LEE KUM KEE Soy Sauce for 30 minutes.

2. Heat stovetop grill pan or skillet over medium-high heat. Add margarine; grill or pan-fry salmon until slightly browned. Turn salmon over and brown other side. When almost done, brush with LEE KUM KEE Plum Sauce. Serve with Sriracha Chili Sauce. *Makes 4 servings*

Broiled Hunan Fish Fillets

3 tablespoons reduced-sodium soy sauce
1 tablespoon finely chopped green onion
2 teaspoons dark sesame oil
1 clove garlic, minced
1 teaspoon minced fresh ginger
¼ teaspoon red pepper flakes
1 pound red snapper, scrod or cod fillets

1. Combine soy sauce, green onion, oil, garlic, ginger and red pepper flakes in small bowl.

2. Spray rack of broiler pan with nonstick cooking spray. Place fish on rack; brush with soy sauce mixture.

3. Broil 4 to 5 inches from heat 10 minutes or until fish flakes easily when tested with fork. *Makes 4 servings*

Orange Almond Scallops

3 tablespoons orange juice
1 tablespoon reduced-sodium soy sauce
1 clove garlic, minced
1 pound bay scallops or halved sea scallops
1 tablespoon cornstarch
2 teaspoons vegetable oil, divided
1 green bell pepper, cut into short, thin strips
1 can (8 ounces) sliced water chestnuts, drained and rinsed
3 tablespoons toasted blanched almonds
3 cups cooked white rice
½ teaspoon finely grated orange peel

1. Combine orange juice, soy sauce and garlic in medium bowl. Add scallops; toss to coat. Marinate at room temperature 15 minutes or cover and refrigerate up to 1 hour.

2. Drain scallops; reserve marinade. Blend marinade into cornstarch in small bowl until smooth.

3. Heat 1 teaspoon oil in wok or large nonstick skillet over medium heat. Add scallops; stir-fry 2 minutes or until scallops are opaque. Remove and reserve.

4. Add remaining 1 teaspoon oil to wok. Add bell pepper and water chestnuts; stir-fry 3 minutes.

5. Return scallops along with any accumulated juices to wok. Stir marinade mixture and add to wok. Cook 1 minute or until sauce boils and thickens. Stir in almonds. Serve over rice. Sprinkle with orange peel. Garnish, if desired. *Makes 4 servings*

Szechuan Seafood Stir-Fry

1 package (10 ounces) fresh spinach leaves
4 teaspoons dark sesame oil, divided
4 cloves garlic, minced, divided
¼ cup reduced-sodium soy sauce
1 tablespoon dry sherry or sake
1 tablespoon cornstarch
1 medium red bell pepper, cut into thin 1-inch-long strips
1½ teaspoons minced fresh ginger
¾ pound peeled deveined large raw shrimp, thawed if frozen
½ pound fresh bay scallops
2 teaspoons sesame seeds, toasted

1. Rinse spinach in cold water; drain. Heat 2 teaspoons oil in large saucepan over medium heat. Add 2 cloves garlic; stir-fry 1 minute. Add spinach; cover and steam 4 to 5 minutes or until spinach is wilted, turning with tongs after 3 minutes. Remove from heat; keep warm.

2. Meanwhile, combine soy sauce, sherry and cornstarch in small bowl; stir until smooth. Heat remaining 2 teaspoons oil in wok or large nonstick skillet over medium-high heat. Add bell pepper; stir-fry 2 minutes. Add remaining 2 cloves garlic and ginger; stir-fry 1 minute. Add shrimp; stir-fry 2 minutes. Add scallops; stir-fry 1 minute or until shrimp and scallops are opaque and cooked through. Add reserved soy sauce mixture; cook 1 minute or until sauce thickens.

3. Transfer spinach mixture to 4 individual plates. Top with seafood stir-fry; sprinkle with sesame seeds.   *Makes 4 servings*

*Tips

Larger, less expensive sea scallops can be substituted for the bay scallops; simply cut them into quarters. One large head of bok choy, thinly sliced, can be substituted for the spinach. Increase steaming the time to 8 minutes or until the bok choy is tender.

Beijing Fillet of
Sole

2 tablespoons reduced-sodium soy sauce
2 teaspoons dark sesame oil
4 sole fillets (6 ounces each)
1¼ cups preshredded cabbage or coleslaw mix
½ cup crushed chow mein noodles
1 egg white, lightly beaten
2 teaspoons sesame seeds
**1 package (10 ounces) frozen snow peas, cooked and
   drained**

1. Preheat oven to 350°F. Combine soy sauce and oil in small bowl. Place fish in shallow dish. Lightly brush both sides of fish with soy sauce mixture.

2. Combine cabbage, noodles, egg white and remaining soy sauce mixture in small bowl. Spoon evenly over each fillet. Roll up fillets. Place, seam side down, in shallow foil-lined roasting pan.

3. Sprinkle rolls with sesame seeds. Bake 25 to 30 minutes or until fish flakes when tested with fork. Serve with snow peas.   *Makes 4 servings*

Seafood & Vegetable Stir-Fry

  2 teaspoons olive oil
  ½ medium red or yellow bell pepper, cut into strips
  ½ medium onion, cut into wedges
10 snow peas, trimmed and cut diagonally into halves
  1 clove garlic, minced
  6 ounces frozen cooked medium shrimp, thawed
  2 tablespoons stir-fry sauce
    Hot cooked rice

1. Heat oil in large nonstick skillet over medium-high heat. Add vegetables; stir-fry 4 minutes. Add garlic; stir-fry 1 minute or until vegetables are crisp-tender.

2. Add shrimp and stir-fry sauce; stir-fry 1 to 2 minutes or until hot. Serve over rice. *Makes 2 servings*

Garlic Prawns with Green Onion

Prep Time: 15 minutes • **Cook Time:** 10 minutes

2 tablespoons cooking oil
1 tablespoon LEE KUM KEE® Minced Garlic
8 ounces prawns, deveined and patted dry
2 tablespoons LEE KUM KEE® Soy Sauce
2 red chili peppers, cut into thin strips
2 green onions, chopped
1 tablespoon LEE KUM KEE® Pure Sesame Oil

1. Heat wok or skillet over high heat until hot. Add cooking oil, LEE KUM KEE Minced Garlic, prawns and LEE KUM KEE Soy Sauce; stir-fry until prawns turn pink.

2. Add chili peppers, green onions and LEE KUM KEE Pure Sesame Oil; cook 1 minute. Transfer to plate and serve immediately. *Makes 2 servings*

Sweet & Sour Seafood Sauté

1 tablespoon vegetable oil
12 ounces raw sea scallops or shrimp, peeled and deveined
1 cup bell pepper strips
1 cup unsweetened pineapple chunks
½ cup canned bamboo shoots, drained
½ cup sweet and sour sauce
Hot cooked rice

Heat oil in wok or large nonstick skillet; add scallops and bell pepper. Sauté 3 to 5 minutes or until scallops are opaque (or shrimp is pink). Add pineapple, bamboo shoots and sweet and sour sauce; cook 3 to 5 minutes or until heated through. Serve over hot rice.   *Makes 4 servings*

Favorite recipe from **National Fisheries Institute**

Shrimp Fried Rice

1 egg
1 egg white
1 tablespoon *plus* 2 teaspoons peanut oil, divided
3 cups chilled cooked white rice
2 tablespoons stir-fry sauce
1 cup small cooked shrimp*
½ cup frozen baby peas or drained canned peas
½ cup thinly sliced green onions

*Or, substitute 1 cup diced cooked pork, beef or chicken.

1. Beat egg with egg white in small bowl. Heat large nonstick skillet over medium-high heat. Add 2 teaspoons oil; heat until hot. Add eggs, tilting skillet to coat surface. Cook 2 minutes or until eggs are set and lightly browned on bottom. Transfer to plate; cut into short, thin strips.

2. Heat remaining 1 tablespoon oil in skillet. Add rice and stir-fry sauce; mix well. Stir in shrimp, peas and onions; heat through. Gently stir egg strips into rice mixture; heat through.   *Makes 2 main-dish servings*

Cellophane Noodle Salad

1 package (about 4 ounces) cellophane* noodles
2 tablespoons peanut or vegetable oil
8 ounces medium or large raw shrimp, peeled and deveined
3 cloves garlic, minced
¼ teaspoon red pepper flakes
½ cup cooked pork or ham strips (optional)
2 tablespoons soy sauce
1 tablespoon fresh lemon juice
1 tablespoon rice vinegar
1 tablespoon dark sesame oil
**⅓ cup thinly sliced green onions or coarsely chopped fresh
    cilantro**

*Cellophane noodles are available in the Asian section of most supermarkets. They are also called bean thread or glass noodles.

1. Place cellophane noodles in medium bowl; cover with warm water. Soak 15 minutes to soften. Drain well; cut into 2-inch pieces.

2. Meanwhile, heat wok or large skillet over medium-high heat. Add peanut oil; heat until hot. Add shrimp, garlic and red pepper flakes; stir-fry 2 minutes. Add pork, soy sauce, lemon juice, vinegar and sesame oil; stir-fry 1 minute.

3. Add cellophane noodles; stir-fry 1 minute or until heated through. Serve warm, chilled or at room temperature. Sprinkle with green onions before serving. *Makes 4 servings*

Steamed Fish Fillets with Black Bean Sauce

1½ pounds white-fleshed fish fillets (Lake Superior whitefish, halibut, rainbow trout or catfish)
1 tablespoon vegetable oil
2 green onions, chopped
2 tablespoons chopped fresh ginger
2 tablespoons black bean sauce (see Note)
Hot cooked rice (optional)
Green onion slivers (optional)

1. Fill large saucepan about one-third full with water. Place bamboo steamer basket over saucepan. Or, fill wok fitted with rack about one-third full with water. Cover and bring water to a boil. Place fillets in single layer on platter that fits into steamer or wok.

2. Heat oil in small skillet until hot. Add green onions, ginger and black bean sauce; stir-fry about 30 seconds or just until fragrant.

3. Immediately pour contents of skillet evenly over fillets. Place platter in steamer; cover and steam 10 to 15 minutes or until fish is tender and flaky. Serve fillets and sauce over rice, if desired. Garnish with green onions.
Makes 4 servings

Note: Jarred black bean sauce is sold in the Asian food section of most large supermarkets. It is made of fermented black soybeans, soy sauce, garlic, sherry, sesame oil and ginger. Black soybeans have a pungent odor and a unique, pronounced flavor. Do not substitute regular black beans.

Spicy Shrimp & Vegetables

6 ounces uncooked spaghetti or Chinese noodles
¾ pound large raw shrimp, peeled and deveined
¼ cup reduced-sodium soy sauce
½ teaspoon red pepper flakes
2 teaspoons dark sesame oil
1 cup snow peas
1 red or yellow bell pepper, cut into thin strips
½ cup shredded carrots
2 teaspoons minced fresh ginger
1½ teaspoons minced garlic
3 tablespoons water
2 teaspoons cornstarch
¼ cup thinly sliced green onions or chopped fresh cilantro

1. Cook spaghetti according to package directions. Drain and keep warm.

2. Meanwhile, combine shrimp, soy sauce and red pepper flakes in medium bowl; toss to coat.

3. Heat oil in wok or large nonstick skillet over medium-high heat. Add snow peas, bell pepper, carrots, ginger and garlic; stir-fry 3 minutes. Remove shrimp from marinade, reserving marinade. Add shrimp to wok; stir-fry 2 minutes.

4. Combine water and cornstarch in small bowl; mix well. Add to wok with reserved marinade; stir-fry 2 minutes or until shrimp are pink and opaque and sauce thickens. Serve with spaghetti; sprinkle with green onions. *Makes 4 servings*

Hot and Sour Shrimp

½ **package (½ ounce) dried shiitake or black Chinese mushrooms***
½ **small unpeeled cucumber**
 1 **tablespoon brown sugar**
 2 **teaspoons cornstarch**
 3 **tablespoons rice vinegar**
 2 **tablespoons reduced-sodium soy sauce**
 1 **tablespoon vegetable oil**
 1 **pound medium raw shrimp, peeled and deveined**
 2 **cloves garlic, minced**
 ¼ **teaspoon red pepper flakes**
 1 **large red bell pepper, cut into short, thin strips**
   Hot cooked Chinese egg noodles (optional)

Or substitute ¾ cup sliced fresh mushrooms. Omit step 1.

1. Place mushrooms in small bowl; cover with warm water. Soak 20 minutes to soften. Drain; squeeze out excess water. Discard stems; slice caps.

2. Cut cucumber in half lengthwise; scrape out seeds. Cut crosswise into ¼-inch slices.

3. Combine brown sugar and cornstarch in small bowl. Blend in vinegar and soy sauce until smooth.

4. Heat oil in wok or large nonstick skillet over medium heat. Add shrimp, garlic and red pepper flakes; stir-fry 1 minute. Add mushrooms and bell pepper strips; stir-fry 2 minutes or until shrimp are opaque.

5. Stir vinegar mixture; add to wok. Cook and stir 30 seconds or until sauce boils and thickens. Add cucumber; stir-fry until heated through. Serve over noodles, if desired. *Makes 4 servings*

Easy Seafood Stir-Fry

1 package (1 ounce) dried black Chinese mushrooms*
½ cup reduced-sodium chicken broth
2 tablespoons dry sherry
1 tablespoon reduced-sodium soy sauce
4½ teaspoons cornstarch
2 teaspoons vegetable oil, divided
½ pound bay scallops or halved sea scallops
¼ pound raw medium shrimp, peeled and deveined
2 cloves garlic, minced
6 ounces (2 cups) fresh snow peas, cut diagonally into halves
2 cups hot cooked white rice
¼ cup thinly sliced green onions

*Or substitute 1½ cups sliced fresh mushrooms. Omit step 1.

1. Place mushrooms in small bowl; cover with warm water. Soak 20 minutes to soften. Drain; squeeze out excess water. Discard stems; slice caps.

2. Blend broth, sherry and soy sauce into cornstarch in another small bowl until smooth.

3. Heat 1 teaspoon oil in wok or large nonstick skillet over medium heat. Add scallops, shrimp and garlic; stir-fry 3 minutes or until seafood is opaque. Remove from wok and reserve.

4. Add remaining 1 teaspoon oil to wok. Add mushrooms and snow peas; stir-fry 3 minutes or until snow peas are crisp-tender.

5. Stir broth mixture and add to wok. Cook 2 minutes or until sauce boils and thickens. Return seafood and any accumulated juices to wok; heat through. Serve over rice; sprinkle with green onions.   *Makes 4 servings*

Mongolian Vegetables
(p. 142)

Green Beans and Shiitake
Mushrooms (p. 138)

Asian-Style Vegetable
Stir-Fry (p. 150)

Vegetarian Asian Noodles
with Peanut Sauce (p. 134)

Vegetable Delights

Easy Fried Rice

Prep Time: 10 minutes • **Cook Time:** 10 minutes

¼ **cup BERTOLLI® Olive Oil**
4 cups cooked rice
2 cloves garlic, finely chopped
1 envelope LIPTON® RECIPE SECRETS® Onion Mushroom
   Soup Mix
½ **cup water**
1 tablespoon soy sauce
1 cup frozen peas and carrots, partially thawed
2 eggs, lightly beaten

1. In 12-inch nonstick skillet, heat oil over medium-high heat and cook rice, stirring constantly, 2 minutes or until heated through. Stir in garlic.

2. Stir in soup mix blended with water and soy sauce and cook 1 minute. Stir in peas and carrots and cook 2 minutes or until heated through.

3. Make a well in center of rice and quickly stir in eggs until cooked.

Makes 4 servings

Szechuan Eggplant

1 pound Oriental eggplants or regular eggplant, peeled
2 tablespoons peanut or vegetable oil
2 cloves garlic, minced
¼ **teaspoon red pepper flakes** *or* ½ **teaspoon hot chili oil**
3 green onions, cut into 1-inch pieces
¼ **cup hoisin sauce**
¼ **cup chicken or vegetable broth**
   Toasted sesame seeds (optional)

Cut eggplants into ½-inch slices; cut slices into 2×½-inch strips. Heat oil in large nonstick skillet over medium-high heat until hot. Add eggplant, garlic and red pepper flakes; stir-fry 7 minutes or until very tender and browned. Reduce heat to medium. Add onions, hoisin sauce and broth; cook 2 minutes. Sprinkle with sesame seeds. *Makes 4 to 6 servings*

Vegetarian Asian Noodles with Peanut Sauce

½ **package (about 9 ounces) uncooked udon noodles*** *or*
   4 ounces uncooked whole wheat spaghetti
1 **tablespoon vegetable oil**
2 **cups fresh snow peas, sliced diagonally into bite-size**
   pieces
1 **cup shredded carrots**
¼ **cup hot water**
¼ **cup peanut butter**
¼ **cup chopped green onions**
2 **to 4 tablespoons hot chili sauce with garlic**
1 **tablespoon soy sauce**
¼ **cup dry-roasted peanuts**

*Udon noodles, made from wheat flour, are usually available in the Asian section of natural food stores or larger supermarkets.

1. Cook noodles according to package directions; drain.

2. Heat oil in large skillet over medium-high heat. Add snow peas and carrots; stir-fry 2 minutes. Remove from heat.

3. Add water, peanut butter, green onions, chili sauce and soy sauce; mix well. Stir in noodles; toss to coat. Sprinkle with peanuts. Serve warm or at room temperature.   *Makes 4 servings*

*Tips

To save time, use packaged shredded carrots. Or for a variation, use a packaged broccoli or coleslaw mix instead of the carrots.

Cantonese Rice Cake Patties

2 cups chilled cooked white rice
⅓ cup chopped red bell pepper
¼ cup thinly sliced green onions
2 egg whites, lightly beaten
1 egg, lightly beaten
2 tablespoons soy sauce
3 tablespoons peanut or vegetable oil, divided

1. Mix rice, bell pepper, green onions, egg whites, egg and soy sauce in medium bowl.

2. Heat large nonstick skillet over medium heat. Add 1 tablespoon oil; heat until hot. For each patty, spoon ⅓ cup rice mixture into skillet; flatten slightly with back of spatula. Cook patties, 3 at a time, 3 to 4 minutes per side or until golden brown. Keep patties warm in 200°F oven. Repeat with remaining oil and rice mixture. *Makes about about 9 patties*

Egg Noodles with Oyster Sauce and Green Onions

½ cup beef or vegetable broth
2 tablespoons oyster sauce
1 tablespoon soy sauce
¼ teaspoon red pepper flakes
6 ounces Chinese egg noodles or vermicelli, cooked and drained
2 green onions, cut into short, thin strips
2 teaspoons dark sesame oil

1. Heat broth, oyster sauce, soy sauce and red pepper flakes in medium saucepan over medium heat. Add noodles; heat through.

2. Stir in green onions and oil. Serve warm, chilled or at room temperature.
Makes 4 servings

Moo Shu Vegetables

½ **package dried Chinese black mushrooms (6 or 7 mushrooms)**
2 **tablespoons vegetable oil**
2 **cloves garlic, minced**
2 **cups shredded napa or green cabbage**
1 **red bell pepper, cut into short, thin strips**
1 **cup fresh or canned bean sprouts, rinsed and drained**
2 **large green onions, cut into short, thin strips**
1 **tablespoon stir-fry sauce**
⅓ **cup plum sauce**
8 **(6-inch) flour tortillas, warmed**

1. Place mushrooms in small bowl; cover with warm water. Soak 20 minutes to soften. Drain; squeeze out excess water. Discard stems; slice caps.

2. Heat oil in wok or large nonstick skillet over medium heat. Add garlic; stir-fry 30 seconds.

3. Add cabbage, mushrooms and bell pepper; stir-fry 3 minutes. Add bean sprouts and green onions; stir-fry 2 minutes. Add stir-fry sauce; stir-fry 30 seconds or until mixture is hot.

4. Spread about 2 teaspoons plum sauce on each tortilla. Spoon heaping ¼ cup vegetable mixture over sauce. Fold bottom of each tortilla up over filling, then fold sides over filling. *Makes 8 servings*

Green Beans and Shiitake Mushrooms

10 to 12 dried shiitake mushrooms (about 1 ounce)
¾ cup water, divided
3 tablespoons oyster sauce
1 tablespoon cornstarch
4 cloves garlic, minced
⅛ teaspoon red pepper flakes
1 tablespoon vegetable oil
¾ to 1 pound fresh green beans, ends trimmed
⅓ cup slivered fresh basil leaves or chopped fresh cilantro
2 green onions, sliced diagonally
⅓ cup roasted peanuts (optional)

1. Place mushrooms in bowl; cover with warm water. Soak 30 minutes to soften. Drain; squeeze out excess water. Discard stems; slice caps into thin strips.

2. Combine ¼ cup water, oyster sauce, cornstarch, garlic and red pepper flakes in small bowl; mix well.

3. Heat wok or medium skillet over medium-high heat. Add oil and swirl to coat surface. Add mushrooms, beans and remaining ½ cup water; cook and stir until water boils. Reduce heat to medium-low; cover and cook 8 to 10 minutes or until beans are crisp-tender, stirring occasionally.

4. Stir cornstarch mixture; add to wok. Cook and stir until sauce thickens and coats beans. (If cooking water has evaporated, add enough water to form thick sauce.) Stir in basil, green onions and peanuts; mix well.

Makes 4 to 6 servings

Oriental Fried Rice

Prep Time: 5 minutes • **Cook Time:** 10 minutes

1 tablespoon vegetable oil
1 egg, beaten
1 box (10 ounces) BIRDS EYE® frozen Seven Vegetable
   Stir-Fry
2 cups cooked rice*
2 tablespoons soy sauce

Need cooked rice in a hurry? Prepare instant white or brown rice, then proceed with recipe.

• Heat 1 teaspoon oil in large skillet over high heat. Add egg; let spread in pan to form flat pancake shape.

• Cook 30 seconds. Turn egg over (egg pancake may break apart); cook 30 seconds more. Remove from skillet; cut into thin strips.

• Remove seasoning pouch from vegetables. Add remaining 2 teaspoons oil to skillet; stir in rice and vegetables.

• Reduce heat to medium-high; cover and cook 5 minutes, stirring twice.

• Add contents of seasoning pouch, soy sauce and cooked egg to skillet; mix well.

• Cook, uncovered, 2 minutes or until heated through.

Makes 2 servings

Mongolian Vegetables

1 package (about 12 ounces) firm tofu, drained
4 tablespoons soy sauce, divided
1 tablespoon dark sesame oil
1 large head bok choy (about 1½ pounds)
2 teaspoons cornstarch
1 tablespoon peanut or vegetable oil
1 large red or yellow bell pepper, cut into short, thin strips
2 cloves garlic, minced
4 small *or* 2 large green onions, cut diagonally into ½-inch pieces
2 teaspoons toasted sesame seeds*

*To toast sesame seeds, spread seeds in small skillet. Shake skillet over medium heat 2 minutes or until seeds begin to pop and turn golden.

1. Press tofu lightly between paper towels; cut into ¾-inch squares or triangles. Place in shallow dish. Combine 2 tablespoons soy sauce and sesame oil; drizzle over tofu. Let stand while preparing vegetables.

2. Cut stems from bok choy leaves; slice stems into ½-inch pieces. Cut leaves crosswise into ½-inch slices.

3. Blend remaining 2 tablespoons soy sauce into cornstarch in cup until smooth.

4. Heat wok or large skillet over medium-high heat. Add peanut oil; heat until hot. Add bok choy stems, bell pepper and garlic; stir-fry 5 minutes. Add green onions and bok choy leaves; stir-fry 2 minutes.

5. Stir soy sauce mixture; add to wok with tofu mixture. Cook 30 seconds or until sauce boils and thickens. Sprinkle with sesame seeds.

Makes 2 main-dish or 4 side-dish servings

Orange-Ginger Tofu & Noodles

⅔ cup orange juice
3 tablespoons reduced-sodium soy sauce
1 clove garlic, minced
½ to 1 teaspoon minced fresh ginger
¼ teaspoon red pepper flakes
5 ounces extra-firm tofu, well drained and cut into
    ½-inch cubes*
1½ teaspoons cornstarch
1 teaspoon canola or peanut oil
2 cups fresh cut-up vegetables, such as broccoli, carrots,
    onion and snow peas
1½ cups hot cooked vermicelli

Tofu must be drained before being stir-fried. Remove any remaining water by placing the block of tofu on several layers of paper towels and covering it with additional paper towels weighted down with a heavy plate. Let it stand for 15 to 20 minutes before cutting into cubes.

1. Combine orange juice, soy sauce, garlic, ginger and red pepper flakes in resealable food storage bag; add tofu. Marinate 20 to 30 minutes. Drain tofu, reserving marinade. Stir marinade into cornstarch until smooth.

2. Heat oil in wok or large nonstick skillet over medium-high heat. Add vegetables; stir-fry 2 to 3 minutes or until vegetables are crisp-tender.

3. Add tofu to wok; stir-fry 1 minute. Stir reserved marinade mixture; add to skillet. Bring to a boil; boil 1 minute. Serve over vermicelli.

Makes 2 servings

Stir-Fried Spinach with Garlic

2 teaspoons peanut or vegetable oil
1 large clove garlic, minced
6 cups packed fresh spinach leaves (about 8 ounces)
2 teaspoons soy sauce
1 teaspoon rice vinegar
¼ teaspoon sugar
1 teaspoon toasted sesame seeds*

*To toast sesame seeds, spread seeds in small skillet. Shake skillet over medium heat 2 minutes or until seeds begin to pop and turn golden.

1. Heat wok or large skillet over medium-high heat. Add oil; heat until hot. Add garlic; cook 1 minute.

2. Add spinach, soy sauce, vinegar and sugar; stir-fry 1 to 2 minutes until spinach is wilted. Sprinkle with sesame seeds.   *Makes 2 servings*

Sesame Noodle Cake

4 ounces vermicelli or Chinese egg noodles
1 tablespoon soy sauce
1 tablespoon peanut or vegetable oil
½ teaspoon dark sesame oil

1. Cook vermicelli according to package directions; drain well. Place in large bowl. Toss with soy sauce until sauce is absorbed.

2. Heat 10- or 11-inch nonstick skillet over medium heat. Add peanut oil; heat until hot. Add vermicelli mixture; pat into even layer with spatula.

3. Cook, uncovered, 6 minutes or until bottom is lightly browned. Invert onto plate, then slide back into skillet, browned side up. Cook 4 minutes or until bottom is well browned. Drizzle with sesame oil. Transfer to serving platter; cut into quarters.   *Makes 4 servings*

Savory Lo Mein

2 tablespoons BERTOLLI® Olive Oil
1 medium clove garlic, finely chopped*
1 small head bok choy, cut into 2-inch pieces
**   (about 5 cups)****
1 envelope LIPTON® RECIPE SECRETS® Onion Soup Mix***
1 cup water
2 tablespoons sherry (optional)
1 teaspoon soy sauce
¼ teaspoon ground ginger (optional)
8 ounces linguine or spaghetti, cooked and drained

*If using LIPTON® Recipe Secrets® Savory Herb with Garlic Soup Mix, omit garlic.

**Or use 5 cups coarsely shredded green cabbage. Decrease 10-minute cook time to 3 minutes.

***Also terrific with LIPTON® RECIPE SECRETS® Onion Mushroom, Savory Herb with Garlic, or Golden Onion Soup Mix.

In 12-inch skillet, heat oil over medium heat and cook garlic and bok choy, stirring frequently, 10 minutes or until crisp-tender. Stir in onion soup mix blended with water, sherry, soy sauce and ginger. Bring to a boil over high heat. Reduce heat to low and simmer uncovered, stirring occasionally, 5 minutes. Toss with hot linguine. Sprinkle, if desired, with toasted sesame seeds.   *Makes about 4 servings*

Chinese Sweet and Sour Vegetables

3 cups broccoli florets
2 medium carrots, diagonally sliced
1 large red bell pepper, cut into short, thin strips
¼ cup water
2 teaspoons cornstarch
1 teaspoon sugar
⅓ cup unsweetened pineapple juice
1 tablespoon soy sauce
1 tablespoon rice vinegar
½ teaspoon dark sesame oil
¼ cup chopped fresh cilantro or sliced green onions (optional)

1. Combine broccoli, carrots and bell pepper in large skillet with tight-fitting lid. Add water; bring to a boil over high heat. Reduce heat to medium; cover and steam 4 minutes or until vegetables are crisp-tender.

2. Meanwhile, combine cornstarch and sugar in small bowl. Blend in pineapple juice, soy sauce and vinegar until smooth.

3. Transfer vegetables to colander; drain. Stir pineapple mixture and add to skillet. Cook and stir 2 minutes or until sauce boils and thickens.

4. Return vegetables to skillet; toss with sauce. Stir in sesame oil. Sprinkle with cilantro.

Makes 4 servings

Asian-Style Vegetable Stir-Fry

¼ **cup honey**
¼ **cup prepared stir-fry sauce**
¼ **to ½ teaspoon crushed red pepper flakes**
4 **teaspoons peanut or vegetable oil**
2 **cups small broccoli florets**
2 **cups small mushrooms**
1 **small onion, cut into wedges and separated into 1-inch strips**
1 **medium carrot, cut diagonally into thin slices**

Combine honey, stir-fry sauce and pepper flakes in small bowl. Heat oil in wok or large skillet over medium-high heat. Add vegetables; cook and stir 2 to 3 minutes or until tender. Add honey mixture; cook and stir about 1 minute or until vegetables are glazed and sauce is bubbly. Serve vegetables over noodles or steamed rice, if desired.   *Makes 4 servings*

Favorite recipe from **National Honey Board**

Cashew Green Beans

1 **tablespoon peanut or vegetable oil**
1 **small onion, cut into thin wedges**
2 **cloves garlic, minced**
1 **package (10 ounces) frozen julienne-cut green beans, thawed, drained and patted dry**
2 **tablespoons oyster sauce**
1 **tablespoon rice vinegar**
1 **tablespoon honey**
¼ **cup coarsely chopped cashews or peanuts**

1. Heat wok or large skillet over medium-high heat. Add oil; heat until hot. Add onion and garlic; stir-fry 3 minutes

2. Add beans; stir-fry 2 minutes. Add oyster sauce, vinegar and honey; stir-fry 1 minute or until heated through. Remove from heat; stir in cashews.   *Makes 4 servings*

Curried
Noodles

7 ounces dried Chinese rice sticks or rice noodles
1 tablespoon peanut or vegetable oil
1 large red bell pepper, cut into short, thin strips
2 large green onions, cut into ½-inch pieces
1 clove garlic, minced
1 teaspoon minced fresh ginger
2 teaspoons curry powder
⅛ to ¼ teaspoon red pepper flakes
½ cup chicken or vegetable broth
2 tablespoons soy sauce

1. Place rice sticks in bowl; cover with warm water. Soak 15 minutes to soften. Drain and cut into 3-inch pieces.

2. Heat wok or large skillet over medium-high heat. Add oil; heat until hot. Add bell pepper; stir-fry 3 minutes.

3. Add green onions, garlic and ginger to wok; stir-fry 1 minute. Add curry powder and red pepper flakes; stir-fry 1 minute.

4. Stir in broth and soy sauce; heat through. Add noodles; cook 3 minutes or until heated through.   *Makes 6 servings*

*Tip
For a spicier noodle dish, use ¼ teaspoon red pepper flakes.

The publisher would like to thank the companies and organizations listed below for the use of their recipes and photographs in this publication.

ACH Food Companies, Inc.

Birds Eye Foods

Crisco is a registered trademark of The J.M. Smucker Company

Del Monte Corporation

Dole Food Company, Inc.

The Golden Grain Company®

Holland House® is a registered trademark of Mott's, LLP

Hormel Foods, LLC

Jennie-O Turkey Store®

Lee Kum Kee (USA) Inc.

MASTERFOODS USA

McIlhenny Company (TABASCO® brand Pepper Sauce)

National Fisheries Institute

National Honey Board

National Onion Association

National Pork Board

Reckitt Benckiser Inc.

Riviana Foods Inc.

The Sugar Association, Inc.

Unilever

USA Rice Federation™

VOLUME MEASUREMENTS (dry)

1/8 teaspoon = 0.5 mL
1/4 teaspoon = 1 mL
1/2 teaspoon = 2 mL
3/4 teaspoon = 4 mL
1 teaspoon = 5 mL
1 tablespoon = 15 mL
2 tablespoons = 30 mL
1/4 cup = 60 mL
1/3 cup = 75 mL
1/2 cup = 125 mL
2/3 cup = 150 mL
3/4 cup = 175 mL
1 cup = 250 mL
2 cups = 1 pint = 500 mL
3 cups = 750 mL
4 cups = 1 quart = 1 L

VOLUME MEASUREMENTS (fluid)

1 fluid ounce (2 tablespoons) = 30 mL
4 fluid ounces (1/2 cup) = 125 mL
8 fluid ounces (1 cup) = 250 mL
12 fluid ounces (1 1/2 cups) = 375 mL
16 fluid ounces (2 cups) = 500 mL

WEIGHTS (mass)

1/2 ounce = 15 g
1 ounce = 30 g
3 ounces = 90 g
4 ounces = 120 g
8 ounces = 225 g
10 ounces = 285 g
12 ounces = 360 g
16 ounces = 1 pound = 450 g

DIMENSIONS

1/16 inch = 2 mm
1/8 inch = 3 mm
1/4 inch = 6 mm
1/2 inch = 1.5 cm
3/4 inch = 2 cm
1 inch = 2.5 cm

OVEN TEMPERATURES

250°F = 120°C
275°F = 140°C
300°F = 150°C
325°F = 160°C
350°F = 180°C
375°F = 190°C
400°F = 200°C
425°F = 220°C
450°F = 230°C

BAKING PAN SIZES

Utensil	Size in Inches/Quarts	Metric Volume	Size in Centimeters
Baking or Cake Pan (square or rectangular)	8×8×2	2 L	20×20×5
	9×9×2	2.5 L	23×23×5
	12×8×2	3 L	30×20×5
	13×9×2	3.5 L	33×23×5
Loaf Pan	8×4×3	1.5 L	20×10×7
	9×5×3	2 L	23×13×7
Round Layer Cake Pan	8×1½	1.2 L	20×4
	9×1½	1.5 L	23×4
Pie Plate	8×1¼	750 mL	20×3
	9×1¼	1 L	23×3
Baking Dish or Casserole	1 quart	1 L	—
	1½ quart	1.5 L	—
	2 quart	2 L	—